AF581111

AS I BECOME

This book contains personal stories and interviews in which individuals discuss their own life experiences, including health struggles and medical interventions. The information presented is intended for general informational and educational purposes only. Neither the author nor the publisher is a licensed medical professional, and nothing in this book should be considered medical advice, diagnosis, or treatment. Readers should not rely on the accounts in this book as a substitute for professional medical advice or care. Always seek the guidance of a qualified physician or other licensed health care provider with any questions you may have regarding your own health, medical conditions, or treatment options.

The author and publisher make no representations or warranties about the accuracy, applicability, or completeness of the information shared by individuals in this book. Reliance on any information provided herein is solely at the reader's own risk. Some names, identifying details, and circumstances may have been changed to protect the privacy of individuals unless they have consented to disclosure.

Published by Greenleaf Book Group Press
Austin, Texas
www.gbgpress.com

Distributed by Greenleaf Book Group

For ordering information or special discounts for bulk purchases, please contact Greenleaf Book Group at PO Box 91869, Austin, TX 78709, 512.891.6100.

Design and composition by Kosuke Shimuta
Cover design by Kosuke Shimuta
Photography by Kosuke Shimuta
Cover image used under license from ©Shutterstock.com
Publisher's Cataloging-in-Publication data is available.

Print ISBN: 979-8-88645-540-3

eBook ISBN: 979-8-88645-541-0

To offset the number of trees consumed in the printing of our books, Greenleaf donates a portion of the proceeds from each printing to the Arbor Day Foundation. Greenleaf Book Group has replaced over 50,000 trees since 2007.

Printed in India by Thomson Press India Private Limited

26 27 28 29 30 31 32 33 10 9 8 7 6 5 4 3 2 1

First Edition

AS I BECOME

A Collection of Life Stories from Japanese Women

Honoring the Japanese women
over fifty whose strength, wisdom,
and resilience shape society.
May their profound insights
continue to inspire the world.

Contents

Now,
I need to
search myself.

Here are twenty-nine stories of soul-searching,
a compilation of interviews
with everyday Japanese women from across generations.
These brave and formidable women searched for
and reclaimed their wellness and happiness.

How do you define *happiness*?

The answer may be different for each person,
but everyone is living their lives every day to the fullest,
in search of their own happiness. Many people say,
"I don't talk about my life; it's not that great."
But when you ask them about their lives from birth to the present,
you will find that they have come through
many turning points of joy and sorrow,
some even experiencing pain so severe that they despair.

Nevertheless, the women featured in this book tell us,
"Now is the most fulfilling time."
Their eyes shine as they say, "I'm looking forward to the rest of my life."

INVEL is an incredible brand
that has improved people's health with fabrics
that generate far-infrared rays,
which is a revolutionary method of promoting nitric oxide production.
They offer scientifically proven products
that cannot be imitated by other companies.

You will encounter crises and setbacks in your life.
What will you think at that time, and how will you overcome it?
What kind of happiness do you envision?

In this era of hundred-year lifespans,
I hope that some of these stories can touch the hearts
of those who are searching for happiness in their future lives.

Miyuki Kushima

Hokkaido

The scenery that can be seen When exiting from a closed world.

The thin wood shavings would dance in the air when my father gently moved his planer. I remember him working as a furniture craftsman in the large entrance of my parents' home in Hakodate, which turned into an instant factory. That's my strongest memory of him—otherwise, I just remember him in his pajamas. He was hospitalized during my elementary school years. When I was in the third grade, he passed away.

After that, my mother raised us three sisters by herself. I withdrew into myself during that time. I was of a retiring nature. My turning point came in sixth grade, when I went for a haircut. The hairdresser said, "Leave it to me; I'll make you pretty." Though I was worried about getting it cut too short, I couldn't insist on my preference and ended up with a very short cut. As I stared anxiously in the mirror, wondering, *What have I done . . .*, the hairdresser asked, "Hey, don't you look amazing?" That moment marked the beginning of my opening to the world. After that, I could even dance to Pink Lady songs with my friends in front of others. In middle school, I threw myself into basketball. Those moments when I'd cut through the defense and change the flow of the game—those were the absolute best.

I started working at a sporting goods store after graduating high school—a job I really enjoyed. Then one day, a respected senior colleague on my floor left the store. She had built up quite a loyal customer base, so I worried, "Nobody's going to visit our floor anymore."

But my boyfriend at the time gave me some perspective, saying, "Miyuki, you can't become that senior colleague, and she can't become you." Those words lifted a weight off my shoulders. When I started focusing on being myself rather than trying to fill someone else's shoes, sure enough, I began building my own loyal customer base, even after we lost my colleague's regular customers.

I married my boyfriend at twenty-five, and we began what seemed like a peaceful life together. But that peace was short-lived. Everything changed when I turned thirty. It started with toe pain after bathing; I thought I'd just bumped something. But days later, I woke up unable to bend my right hand. Then, it was my left hand. Soon after, my right shoulder began to hurt—the pain was so intense it reduced me to tears. The orthopedist suspected something serious and referred me to internal medicine. They ruled out rheumatism initially. But no clear diagnosis came, despite blood tests and X-rays. I reached a point where I couldn't even bathe alone anymore; my husband had to wash me as I stood there helplessly in the bathroom. It was unbearable . . .

I could do nothing but cry. After countless visits to hospitals in Hakodate, I finally went to one in Tokyo. There, a slight anomaly on an X-ray led to what we'd initially ruled out—a diagnosis of rheumatism. By then, two years had passed since my first symptoms. Even with a diagnosis, the pain didn't go away. I withdrew into myself, feeling that healthy people could never understand what I was going through. Yet paradoxically, I stubbornly tried to maintain a normal life, gripping kitchen knives and cutting vegetables with my whole body, turning food preparation into a kind of physical therapy. I think I had a dark expression all the time. Through it all, my husband was there, washing me when I couldn't, carefully wrapping each of my fingers in poultice every night. I couldn't even say "thank you."

During a conversation with a friend, she told me about her sister's struggle. Her husband had a connective tissue disease. "My sister changes his socks every day," she said. "He never says thank you and just sits there with a sullen face."

Her words hit me like a ton of bricks. "My husband's actions are his calling!" I realized. I had been so caught up in feeling that I needed to apologize constantly. That day, for the first time since my rheumatism diagnosis, I finally managed to say "thank you" to my husband.

After that realization, my mindset changed. I started finding creative ways to do what I could. For instance, I discovered that stubborn jar lids could be opened with the right tools, and a faucet could be managed with certain techniques. I also learned to honestly accept what I couldn't do anymore, like letting my husband take over chopping vegetables. Still, my rheumatism continued to progress. By thirty-five, I couldn't even take off a filler from a brand-new shoe, so I decided to change careers.

I started working at a shop that sold mineral accessories. While I wasn't particularly interested at first, once I began studying, I found it fascinating. Around that time, my husband's friend introduced me to working with Invel products. Though he didn't know about my condition, I thought, *This might be something I can do* and decided to give it a try. I started by purchasing some products to learn about them. What happened next was miraculous—I, who had difficulty walking, could run after wearing the Invel spats for a while! Then came the multi-belt. I wrapped it around my fingers, and the pain subsided by the next morning. Regular medications had stopped working by then, and this felt like my last ray of hope after trying all the new drugs.

Just days after experiencing these miracles, the Great East Japan Earthquake struck. Hakodate was hit hard. While my family and home were fortunately safe, our accessory shop near the coast was damaged by the tsunami . . . I had no time to say I couldn't wring out the rag; I just needed to throw myself into recovery efforts. This was only possible thanks to the Invel products, which had arrived just days before.

Today, I'm the manager of that shop, and I'm actively involved in activities with INVEL too. While I'm not completely pain-free and still need monthly injections, INVEL has given me back a body that can move again. After being immobile for so long, I just can't help wanting to move, wanting to jump around—I simply can't stay still! That's why my dream for the future is to travel the world with INVEL. Having experienced what it's like to be trapped in my own shell, I think I can understand the feelings of others in similar situations. I want to journey with them to see the beautiful view that appears when we finally step out of that closed world.

Miyuki Kushima _01

The scenery that can be seen
When exiting from a closed world.

Miyuki Kushima_01

Masumi Kurishita

Hokkaido

Surrounded by smiles and happiness, Youth is just within reach.

"She could cry for thirty-six hours in a day," this is how my mother used to describe me. I was that kind of withdrawn child. Though she'd say such things, she was incredibly kind, and I loved her dearly.

Our family ran what was then called a *yorozu-ya*, a general store, selling daily necessities. Being "the shop owner's daughter" meant I was often under public scrutiny, and the rules of etiquette were strict, especially since my mother was a tea ceremony instructor. I was constantly reminded to say "thank you" and maintain a smile. While I struggled to be a "good child," I never really understood what that meant. I just focused on not doing anything embarrassing. This mindset kept me introverted throughout elementary and middle school.

But at my middle school graduation, my homeroom teacher told me something that changed everything: "People around you will recognize your wonderful character. The more they try to get to know you, the more they will realize how amazing you are. Keep believing in what you believe in. If you find even one person who truly understands you, your world will expand."

Those words were eye-opening. Gradually, my life began to change. I went to a girls' high school away from my neighborhood, where I was no longer just "the shop owner's daughter." My personality did a complete 180-degree turn; I actively participated in volunteer work, and my horizons began to broaden.

I enrolled in a junior college in Tokyo. But right around graduation, my father suddenly passed away. I hadn't been home in ages, and even though it was around my coming-of-age ceremony, I couldn't make it back for that either. When I finally went to see him, there was a *furisode* (a type of traditional kimono that is worn by young, unmarried women) by his pillow. He had prepared this special ensemble for my coming-of-age ceremony. It broke my heart.

My father survived being in a Kamikaze attack unit during the war. I wish I had taken the time to hear more of his stories. Though I had regrets, there was nothing I could do now. As the eldest daughter, I decided to return to Hokkaido to support the family, but neither my mother nor our relatives seemed to expect this of me. They just shrugged it off.

When I dropped out of college, I ended up going back to Tokyo. There, I married my first husband—he was two years younger than me, just eighteen, someone I met at my part-time job. Maybe we were both just caught up in youthful passion. Our income was unstable, and life quickly became difficult. I returned to Hokkaido for my father's first death anniversary, but I felt out of place.

Finally, having decided to work in Hokkaido again, I took sales positions at children's clothing stores and jewelry shops. Being a merchant's daughter, I had a natural affinity for sales, and there was so much to learn. At thirty, I married for the second time. He was introduced to me through my younger sister's friend. But ironically, the woman who made the introduction started meddling in my husband's affairs. The phone would ring every hour after I got home, and I even received messages saying, "Your husband was at some woman's house." I was determined not to give up, but eventually, I became exhausted. Looking back now, it was like something out of a soap opera.

After that period, I worked in insurance sales and restaurants. My third and current husband was a customer at the restaurant; he's in the Self-Defense Forces and eleven years younger than me. When we met, despite the age gap, I hadn't realized just how much younger he was. We have three children together, plus two from previous marriages, so we're quite a large family. We were struggling financially, and the 2011 Great East Japan Earthquake dealt another blow to our lives. I had been working as a regular employee at a fast-food franchise for seventeen years when suddenly, I decided to quit.

Looking back now, perhaps it was fate pushing me toward resignation. All of Japan was going through severe economic hardship then. My husband was away for about half a year helping with reconstruction efforts, but his salary was reduced. We were just an ordinary family getting by, but eventually, we couldn't manage anymore and had to undergo debt consolidation. We even had to give up our mortgaged house. I learned the hard way that there are no guarantees in what we consider a normal life. I thought I knew, but I realized that the truth is different.

One day, a mom from a group took me to an Invel dome salon. I experienced "Silky," the hydrogen water generator. At the time, both my eldest and second daughters suffered from atopic dermatitis, and I'm embarrassed to say that, financially, I couldn't give them the medical treatment they needed. But Silky helped, and they didn't have to go to the hospital after all!

To be honest, at first, I thought that all the products were too expensive, but I realized that wasn't the case. I was also taken to a seminar, and everyone there was beautiful and lively, even though they were older than me. I still remember that a ninety-four-year-old cheerfully declared, "I have six more years of youth until I'm a hundred!" I realized that I was still a novice.

I have an unfulfilled dream from my youth. I've always loved reading, and I've consistently wished to read *The Pillow Book* and *The Tale of Genji* in their original classical Japanese. Of course, reading these original texts requires some scholarly knowledge. That's why I need that time, that leisure. Yes, I want to return to university. Being here, I believe that dream will come true someday. Especially in this place, filled with people who have found their happiness, where smiles and joy overflow.

Masumi Kurishita_02

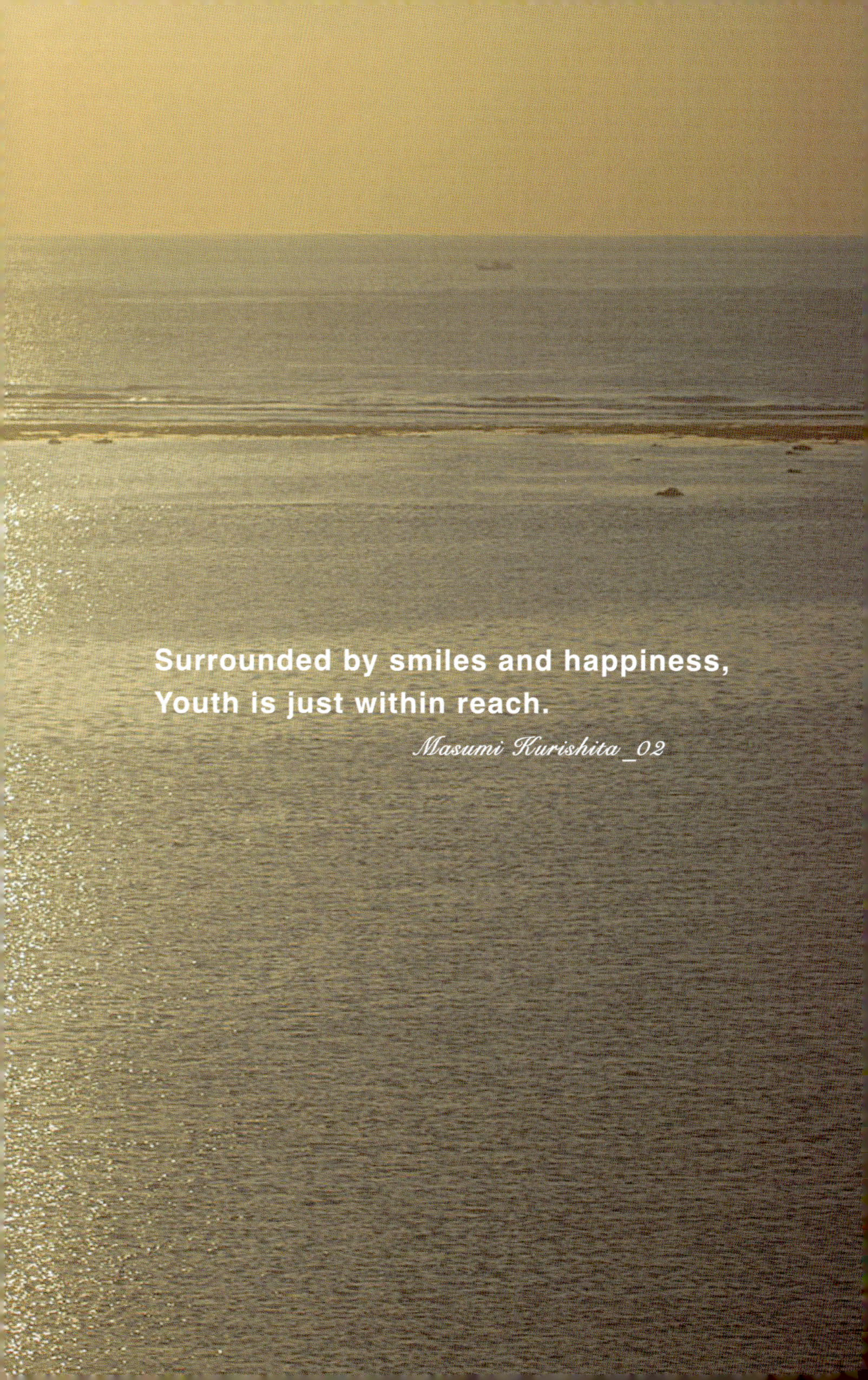

Surrounded by smiles and happiness,
Youth is just within reach.

Masumi Kurishita_02

Miyuki Murosaki

Hokkaido

A warmed body and heart Have brought happiness along.

I'd come home completely soaked from playing in the snow. Growing up in Nakafurano-cho, Hokkaido, I was an energetic child who loved climbing snowy mountains for fun. I often helped my parents with their farm work, planting and harvesting potatoes. I could find joy in anything and was naturally curious.

During those days, what really captured my heart was the piano. When I saw my kindergarten teacher playing the organ, I thought, *That's amazing!* However, in Nakafurano-cho, we didn't have any piano teachers nearby. My hardworking parents started taking me to piano lessons when I was in fourth grade. My sister and I went together, and I was overjoyed when they even put a piano in our home. I kept up with lessons until my first year of high school.

I majored in business studies in high school and then started working at a restaurant in Furano after graduation. During lavender season, we'd be completely packed with tourists. It was there that I suddenly became too shy to welcome them. It took me two or three months just to be able to properly say, "welcome."

Though I struggled quite a bit, after five years, I worked my way up to a leadership position. However, as more young staff joined, I began to feel the generational shift and made a career change to an administrator managing agricultural land improvement. Around that time, I met my first husband through a friend. In Furano, everyone typically marries in their early twenties, so maybe I felt rushed.

After marriage, whether due to personality differences or not, I felt restricted. We divorced five years later, when I was twenty-nine. Afterward, through my sister, who worked in administration and nursing, I became a nursing assistant. Despite the challenges of night shifts, it was rewarding to work where I could truly feel I was helping others.

At thirty-five, I moved to Sapporo. When my boyfriend got a job transfer, we decided to get married. When we first met through a mutual friend, I thought he was someone whose expression never changed. Because that was my first impression, I always spoke to him naturally, without putting on airs. He found that interesting. As we started seeing each other more, I discovered I could bring out different expressions in him, which made me happy, too.

I started seeing even more of my husband's smiles after our daughter was born. I was touched, thinking, *I didn't know he could make such expressions!* But around that time, a business his father had guaranteed went bankrupt. We had to move in with my in-laws. There were some tensions with my mother-in-law, and it was quite challenging. Needing some space, I started working part-time in nursing care. During this period, I was also struggling with secondary infertility. Though I pursued treatment, when I turned forty, I thought *Enough* and decided to stop.

I was forty-four when I discovered INVEL. I noticed the logo on a glove my friend was using. When I asked about it and tried it on, I felt warmth. Remembering my mother's complaints about hand pain, I bought some for her. When the product arrived, the Invel distributors taught me various things, and not only was the product excellent, but the person explaining it had this radiant energy. The product helped relieve my mother's hand pain. When I tried it myself, I first noticed my body temperature increasing. I'd always had a very low body temperature, normally around 35 degrees. But it gradually rose to about 36 degrees. Then, six months after discovering INVEL, at age forty-four, I became pregnant and gave birth to a son! My husband's smiles grew even broader after that.

With young children and caring for my father-in-law, I couldn't fully engage with Invel activities right away. But as the world changed and online communication became normal, someone suggested, "You could do this online." That's when I started focusing on digital outreach.

While caring for both in-laws, I had another significant encounter. The husband of a daycare company representative was struggling with cirrhosis. When I introduced the representative to INVEL, her husband's condition improved. Thanks to her connections—she was powerful and inspiring—my network grew significantly. We worked together toward higher titles, and with her support, I finally advanced to "INVEList." (For Invel distributors, this is the first leadership title they strive for.) She's become a trusted partner who walks this path with me.

Recently, one of our friends shared the wonderful news of achieving their long-awaited pregnancy! While infertility is difficult to discuss openly, there are so many people struggling with it. I want to help them. Through my experiences, I've learned that health truly is everything—not just regarding infertility. When your whole family is healthy, that's when you can truly feel happiness.

I've been fortunate to find this happiness through INVEL. That's why I want to bring both health and financial prosperity to more people. I've made my decision: In 2025, I'm going to open a dome salon in Nakafurano-cho. I want to share this experience of being surrounded by love and light with as many people as possible. That's my commitment.

Miyuki Murosaki_03

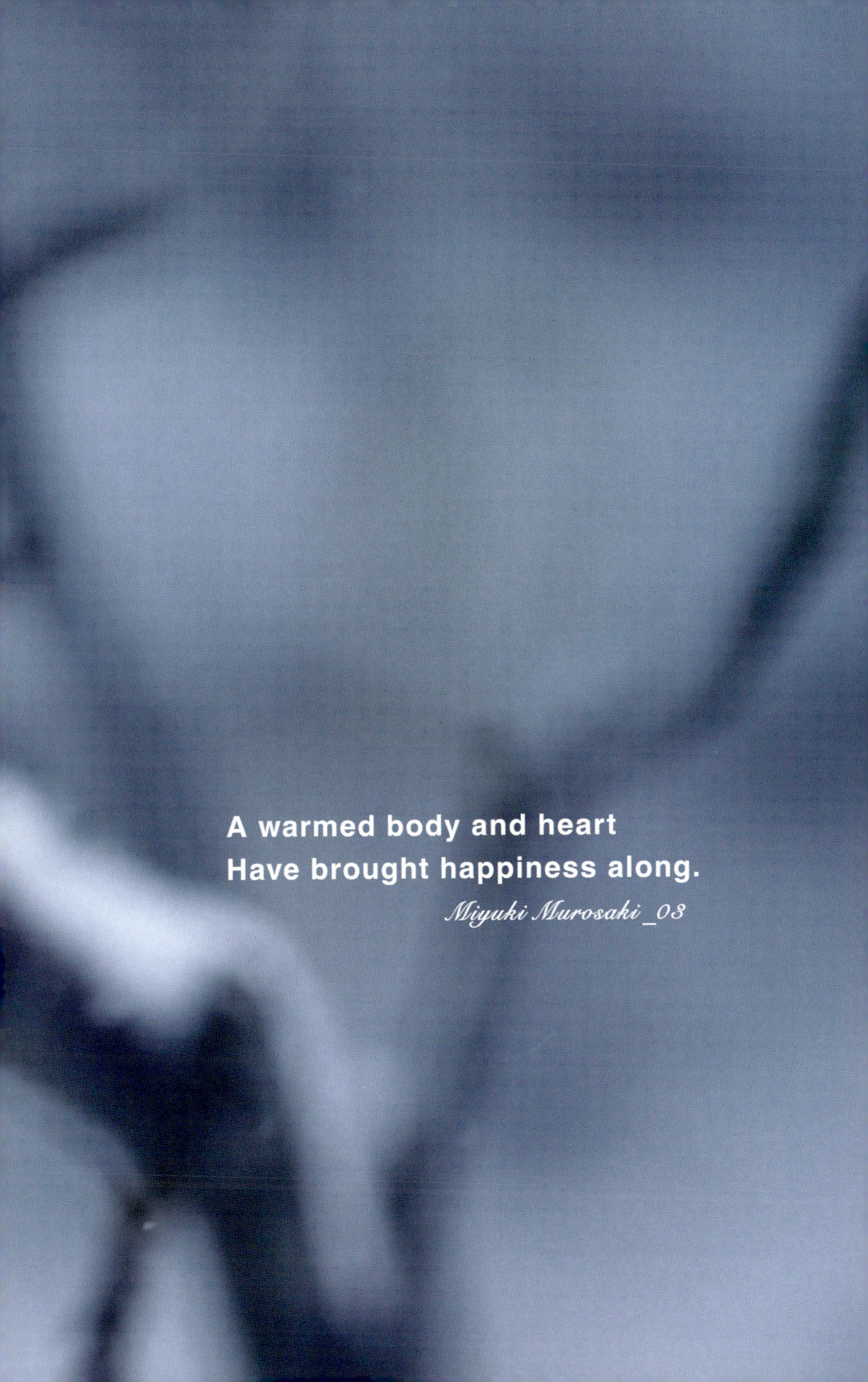

A warmed body and heart
Have brought happiness along.

Miyuki Murosaki_03

Chizuru Konuma

Hokkaido

I'm feeling completely fulfilled right now. Because of those eight years That I now see as my training period.

My father worked for a life insurance company, which meant my childhood was spent moving all around the country. From Hokkaido to Gunma, Hiroshima, and Mie—our whole family would relocate together for each new posting.

While changing schools was daunting at first, I gradually got used to it. Our family of four was really close, so wherever we were posted, we'd make the most of it by visiting local tourist spots on weekends. We actually came to enjoy this nomadic school life. As a child, I dreamed of becoming an electronic organ teacher. I switched to piano later on and kept at it consistently for about twenty years. But I was never the type to stay cooped up indoors—quite the opposite!

I joined the tennis club in middle and high school, getting thoroughly tanned from morning to evening practice. During lunch breaks, I'd be out, pulling the roller across the tennis courts. After classes, it was straight to club activities, and once that was done, I'd sit down at the piano with that same disciplined posture.

By high school, though, I was getting weary of our nomadic lifestyle. The area we were living in at the time was particularly cold, which might have made it harder. I wanted to return to Hakodate, my birthplace. After seeing a poster of Hakodate's stunning night view, I was captivated and decided to make it my home.

After high school graduation, I left my family for the first time and moved to Hakodate alone. While studying early childhood education at junior college, I started working part-time as a piano instructor at a music school. After graduation, I took a full-time position at the same school, where I continued teaching until I was forty. I met my current husband at twenty-eight, through a friend's introduction. The moment we met, I had an intuition that he might be "the one."

Now we have two daughters and live peaceful days. Looking at my life story, there's not much drama or hardship. But there was one event that changed everything—my encounter with network business.

It started at a student recital. As an instructor, I would always dress formally and take photos with my students at these events, but I hated how I looked in those pictures. I had been wanting to lose weight when my husband brought home a diet protein that a client had recommended. It turned out to be a network marketing product. Initially, I was more interested in the product than the business opportunity, but after attending a seminar, something clicked! Given that my piano teaching job often came with unexpected expenses and constant financial struggles, I felt motivated to give it a try.

The biggest eye-opener was attending that network business's international event. The venue was filled with thousands of members from around the world, pulsing with loud music and brilliant lights. I was completely overwhelmed by the power of the people on stage and the spectacular atmosphere. After that, I was hooked on network marketing.

Looking back now, though, I realize those eight years with the previous network business were like training. While the products were good, the business structure wasn't quite right. No matter how hard I worked, I couldn't save any money. Then, a leader from the same group told me, "Something incredible is coming!"—that was INVEL.

When I touched the card, something instantly clicked. Initially, I ran both businesses in parallel, but after receiving a 400,000 yen deposit in my fourth month with INVEL, I switched over completely. The reliability of the income structure was totally different. Plus, Invel products are everyday essentials like clothing and bedding, things people will always need.

"Just wear it, just sleep with it"—it's simple to use and easy to recommend, and you can feel the effects quickly! Unlike food products, there's no worry about expiration dates or expense issues, as you need to have additional products for your sampling activities. It's simple, convenient, reliable, and safe.

At that time, my older daughter was going through a rebellious phase, and I was hoping to spend more time with family, so choosing INVEL was an easy decision. Though I'm usually not a very confident person, I found I could be truly confident about Invel products. Being able to recommend them naturally and confidently to others was a huge draw.

It's been fifteen years now. To others, my journey might look smooth and successful. Of course, after being in this business for so long, I've faced challenges with interpersonal relationships and compatibility issues—that's inevitable. But thanks to INVEL, I've learned the importance of believing in myself and discovered the power that comes from that self-belief. This has helped me grow into someone others can trust.

Looking back, I realize that INVEL is truly the perfect place for lifelong learning and expanding one's horizons. Moving forward, my goal is to share Invel's wonderful products and business opportunities with as many people as possible. I hope to help create a world where each person can achieve mental, physical, and financial well-being, living true to themselves with genuine smiles on their faces.

Chizuru Konuma_04

I'm feeling completely fulfilled right now.
Because of those eight years
That I now see as my training period.

Chizuru Konuma_04

Miho Matsuya

Hokkaido

From teatime, Happiness spreads Throughout the world.

I was the kind of kid who would play softball before school and volleyball after—always on the move. Growing up in Otaru, Hokkaido, winters meant skiing, though I'd sometimes get myself into trouble by venturing into dangerous areas, causing worry for the rescue teams.

I had a great relationship with my parents and brother, growing up so carefree you might call me happy-go-lucky. Even in those early days, I had an especially strong desire to "be of help to others." When I visited the police station during a high school extracurricular activity, something clicked, and I thought, *This is it!* After graduation, I joined the Hokkaido Police Force.

Around that time, a female Osaka police officer had won a silver medal in Olympic shooting, which created momentum for strengthening shooting programs within the police force. That's when they approached me during my community police duty assignment. I joined the team and trained hard, but found myself drawn to our team captain, who was ten years my senior. I took the plunge to make the first move, and now he's my husband. Since I was still quite young, I waited for the right time and got married at twenty-two.

After marriage, I continued both my police work and shooting career. I was even selected as an Olympic trainee. When I had my first daughter, I took a full year of maternity leave, but after returning to work, I still had five to six competitions annually, often being away from home for two weeks at a time. My husband would take care of our child during these periods.

Like Olympic medalist Ryoko Tani, I aimed to win gold as a mother and pursued this goal with determination. While I managed to compete in national and international competitions, when I had my second daughter at twenty-nine, I started feeling that I wanted to be present for these precious moments with my children. I wanted them to have more siblings, and considering the frequent transfers required in the Hokkaido Police Force and thinking about our family's future—particularly how many children we could raise while both working—I decided to resign.

Later, I had two more daughters, creating a lively household. But as children grow, so do expenses. When our eldest decided to enroll at a middle school in Tokyo, we needed money for tuition and living costs. Add to that my husband's job transfer and a house replacement, and our budgets got tight. In my younger days as a civil servant, I hadn't worried much about money, but now I truly felt its importance. I wondered what I could do to help.

I wanted to build a career and increase our income, so I became an instructor at a major cram school. Though I was assigned one class, my income couldn't cover payroll for an additional teacher. So I determined to run the school by myself. I'd spend hours after school marking tests of my students, then preparing for the next day, working until 2 or 3 a.m., then waking up at 5 or 6 a.m. to make breakfast and lunch boxes for my elementary and middle school children. I was exhausted beyond sleep, and my health deteriorated to the point where I couldn't eat. I'd hit rock bottom. Seeing my condition, a nurse friend gave me a white stole, saying, "Try wearing this." It was an Invel product. Wearing it felt surprisingly good, and I didn't want to take it off. When I started using the mat and blanket too, I could finally sleep! When they suggested I become a distributor, I was skeptical, thinking that the products only worked for me, who worked as a tough police officer. But then, my nurse friend and a doctor's wife explained the clinical data to me. Coming from medical professionals, their words carried weight.

I gradually began introducing it to interested mom friends. With four children and running a culture school from home, I had plenty of connections with other mothers. Reactions varied; some were skeptical, like I had been, while others became even more enthusiastic than me. Amusingly, my third daughter, then in fifth grade, was so concerned that she analyzed it from a legal perspective. She's now studying law at university.

Having been skeptical myself at first, I always prioritize honesty when sharing information about INVEL. But discovering INVEL has truly broadened my horizons. I used to think my way was the only right way, but through INVEL, I've learned there are so many different perspectives.

My Invel business is geographically broadened so that my active personality perfectly fits. I'm constantly traveling to seminars around the country. I'm away from home about as much as I was during my shooting competition days. The difference now is that my children are grown and independent in various places, so we meet up when I'm in their areas for seminars.

While I may not have any grand dreams anymore, I want to continue spreading happiness through sharing tea with friends and having meaningful conversations. When sharing INVEL, yes, there's business income, but that's not all. You make precious friends along the way. Each of these connections ripples outward into the world. With this belief, I look forward to enjoying today's teatime as well.

Miho Matsuya_05

From teatime,
Happiness spreads
Throughout the world.
Miho Matsuya _05

Saori Matsuda

Iwate

With peace of mind
Comes the freedom to choose
For a life filled with brilliance and vigor.

I was born in Tōno City, Iwate, a place famous for its folkloric atmosphere, with tales of *kappa* water spirits and *zashiki-warashi* house spirits. Our family has run a shop there since my great-grandfather's time. My grandmother started with a seed shop, which my mother later transformed into a flower shop. My father worked outside the family business, providing us with a stable income.

Growing up in a sprawling valley surrounded by mountains, rivers, and fields, I spent my childhood running through the hills, playing actively alongside the boys. In middle school, I captained both the track and volleyball teams and participated in *ekiden* relay races. I kept up with ekiden after entering the workforce, even winning a competition with my company team. Sports really defined my youth.

In elementary school, I dreamed of becoming a florist. But by middle school, as I began to understand the challenges and behind-the-scenes work of running a flower shop, my enthusiasm wavered. I even declared there wouldn't be a successor to our family business. Though I have a younger sister, our overly familiar neighbors in the valley would always ask, "Which sister will take over? It'll be the older one, right?" These questions left me feeling somewhat defeated.

After high school, I enrolled in a specialized flower school in Tokyo. A one-year program covering everything about flowers seemed perfect. I felt I needed more knowledge before taking over the family business, and I wanted to experience life outside our valley. That year of study flew by. I started working part-time at my training placement and ended up getting hired there. The company was a prestigious florist that mainly served weddings, the Imperial Household, and government offices, and I was assigned to their high-end funeral division. Though I'd planned to return home after a year, I learned so much and enjoyed the work so much that I stayed for three years.

I finally returned home at twenty-three, prompted by my grandfather's illness. My grandmother's health was also failing, and my mother was struggling to manage both the business and caregiving. A year later, my sister came back after finishing university and began helping at my mother's flower shop. Though the family was reunited in Iwate, we faced difficult times.

The Great East Japan Earthquake hit in 2011. While our shop and house suffered minimal damage, being in a disaster area meant there was no market for flowers. During this time, Grandfather's condition deteriorated rapidly. He had Parkinson's disease and was moved to a facility in Kamaishi, but when we reunited after the evacuation period, he was completely exhausted. My grandmother, shocked by his condition, passed away first, and Grandfather followed soon after.

We managed to get by thanks to my father's outside income, but the year after my grandparents passed away, he had a fatal accident while driving a dump truck in the mountains. Despite being airlifted to the hospital, he couldn't be saved. Having lost our main support, we three women—Mother, my sister, and I—faced adversity once again.

With no other options, even if we closed the shop, we decided we had to continue. We consolidated our business by closing the shopping center location and focusing on our home shop. Just when we were managing with help from my uncle who lived with us, he was diagnosed with cancer and began his battle with illness. The misfortunes continued as my mother's health declined too. Then COVID-19 hit, canceling all graduation and entrance ceremonies, and we lost major jobs like venue decorations.

Looking back, though, this became our turning point. We had never taken proper breaks before, but for the first time, I suggested to my mother, "Why don't you go out for a meal with friends?" One of these friends knew about INVEL, noticed my mother wasn't well, and invited her to a dome salon. My mother went alone at first but then told my sister and me, "It's not cheap, so I want to discuss it with family." After trying it ourselves and feeling strongly that my mother should use it, I signed up to become a distributor.

After starting to use INVEL, my mother was able to reduce her medication for her chronic illness. Then, I had my own unexpected experience. Cancer was discovered. I'd felt a lump in my breast since my teens, but since health checkups hadn't flagged anything concerning, I'd mostly ignored it. However, after using INVEL, I noticed the lump getting smaller and mentioned it casually to Mother, who insisted we go to the hospital. The diagnosis was malignant—three years to live if untreated, but treatable with chemotherapy.

I have a partner I want to share my life with, so before starting treatment, I consulted my doctor about having children. Though it was a race against time, when I expressed my desire to have children, the doctor suggested freezing my eggs. I had one chance before starting chemotherapy. Given my age of thirty-five, they said we'd be lucky to get one egg, but amazingly, we harvested ten. Even more remarkably, there was no pain during the procedure, and the eggs had the cellular age of someone in their twenties. This must have been the result of wearing Invel boxer shorts.

Looking back, what I thought was for my mother's benefit might have actually been meant for me. I encountered INVEL just when I needed it for cancer treatment. While chemotherapy usually comes with side effects, I hardly needed any medication to manage them. It also provided crucial financial support: being able to choose expensive treatments without hesitation was thanks to INVEL. There are many Invel members who have overcome illness, and I received so much courage and energy from people who understood what I was going through. Now it's my turn to share.

Based on my personal experience, I want to spread INVEL's wonderfulness to as many people as possible, showing them that you can overcome illness, preserve your dream of having children, and not worry about financial instability.

Saori Matsuda_06

With peace of mind
Comes the freedom to choose
For a life filled with brilliance and vigor.
Saori Matsuda_06

Akemi Matsuo

Hokkaido

The connections from my past Have led to new ones.

My earliest memories are of our family of three—my mother, brother, and me. I'm told my father passed away before I turned two. At his memorial service, I sang my favorite song and "lightened the mood," as my mother tells it.

My mother was raised strictly as the daughter of a station master of Japan National Railways in Hokkaido. Before meeting my father, she had been forced into an arranged marriage by her father. Though she broke free from that and married my father instead, he passed away early. My mother had worked at a National Railways cafeteria, and after his death, she raised us alone.

As a young child, I was often brought to her workplace, where I spent much of my time. Despite all her sacrifices for us, I ended up becoming what you'd call a troubled teen; maybe I went too wild. After middle school, I enrolled in beauty school but dropped out quickly. After that, I bounced between various part-time jobs, working as a waitress at some bars in Susukino (a famous district for hostess bars), and so on.

I met my first husband while working at a coffee shop. We married when I was twenty-two and had two children—a boy and a girl—but his sales career wasn't going well. We also never got along with his parents, so I quickly opted for divorce. Six months later, I married my second husband, who was still quite immature. We had gone to the same kindergarten and reconnected in middle school, remaining friends since then. What started as a joke between us—"If we get divorced, let's marry each other"—came true. We had three children together, but once again, my husband's sales work struggled. He seemed to become a completely different person. So I found myself divorcing again, with five children total, when my youngest was just eight months old.

My priority was feeding my children, so I started job hunting. But finding work with five children was nearly impossible in those days. I even resorted to putting a small white lie on my resume, listing only three children. Finally, I was honest with Duskin, and they hired me for a part-time position. Though I had work, life remained challenging. Each day, I'd send my two older children to elementary school and take the three younger ones to kindergarten. With my youngest in a baby carrier, I'd spend fifteen or twenty minutes cycling to the kindergarten with one child in front and another behind.

I'd then cycle to work, already exhausted from the morning rush. Rainy days were the worst. With no time or money for the bus, I'd throw on a raincoat and pedal through it. One morning, while doing my makeup, one of my children vanished right before my eyes! It was my fourth child, and I couldn't find them anywhere. Following my instincts, I rushed to the kindergarten, and there they were, having followed their elementary school sibling. I nearly fainted from relief. The older siblings were good at watching the younger ones, which must have made them feel confident.

Though we lived in a tiny, dilapidated apartment that even had mice, the time spent there with my children was my sanctuary. It was never peaceful with all the noise, but for my family's sake, I threw myself into work. In sales, I kept pursuing better results. I never took time off, even when the children were sick; I'd just take them along in the company car. That probably wouldn't fly these days. After five years of this desperate effort, I was offered a full-time position and eventually became the sales department manager.

My children grew up properly, never becoming delinquent like I had been. We finally escaped that hand-to-mouth existence. Around that time, I reconciled and remarried my second husband. I was fifty. Being someone who maintains connections once formed, I had kept good relationships with both ex-husbands. We reconciled because he had found stability both at work and personally. He would say things like, "Sorry for the trouble I caused back then." Since he'd been regularly meeting the children, getting back together felt natural.

We were living a peaceful life together when, two years ago, my husband was diagnosed with cirrhosis. There was already fluid accumulation in his abdomen, and doctors gave him just one year to live. But life has mysterious ways of bringing new connections. Through my husband's illness, I discovered INVEL. At the time, I had left Duskin due to workplace relationships and was helping at my brother's chiropractic clinic, which led to a job at a day service center run by someone I met there. While working there, I was recommended Invel products by a client's family who suggested I try it for my husband.

He started with a mat, then got a blanket two months later. Remarkably, all his health indicators started improving! The doctor was astounded, repeatedly saying, "This is incredible!" Recently, we even installed an Invel water server, and now he is using Invel shirts and spats too. Then, despite having alcoholic cirrhosis, my husband felt so good he even tried having a drink! We joke about it—him saying, "It's nothing! I'm saved!" and me replying, "No, don't thank me; thank the Invel mat!"

I reconciled with my once-separated husband, and now we can even joke about such things. It's amazing how these old bonds led me to new ones through INVEL. While I've had my share of hardships, when you take a long view of life, it's like a winding road; you never know where it might lead. Speaking of connections, since joining INVEL, I've experienced so many wonderful chance encounters. Like becoming friends with someone sitting next to me on a plane, then mysteriously meeting her again by chance. Now she's my Invel colleague. This kind of thing has happened several times.

Just recently, I had an especially meaningful encounter; I met Carla, CEO of INVEL! When we hugged, I couldn't stop crying. My current dream is to title-advance to an International INVEList. As a first step, I want to open a salon and take on the challenge of running a business. Actually, I'm dealing with some health issues myself now, triggered by my mother's death. I have Basedow's disease, but it's stable thanks to INVEL. So I'm managing fine. Moving forward, I want to cherish all these connections I've made while pursuing my global ambitions.

Akemi Matsuo_07

The connections from my past
Have led to new ones.

Akemi Matsuo_07

Yuko Chiba

Iwate

Moving forward together with friends, Sharing laughter along the way.

Ever since I was little, I loved having fun with friends, and I was always taking the initiative to throw parties for Christmas and birthdays. I've performed on stage and am comfortable with being in the spotlight. Have you heard of *Shin-buyō*? It's a form of Japanese dance that makes traditional dance more accessible by incorporating folk songs and popular music. I've been practicing it since first grade and continue to this day.

It all started when my mother began taking me to lessons. My mother was a strong woman who would drive tractors and work the fields. My father was a craftsman by nature, often away from home for work. So usually, it was just my mother, my two sisters, and me, growing up in a lively household surrounded by women, including our grandma and great-grandma.

As the eldest daughter, I was expected to eventually return to Iwate, but after high school, I decided to first venture outside the prefecture, becoming a bus guide for a company operating around Izu and Hakone. While I enjoyed the work, after about three years, there was this unspoken expectation to "get married and quit"; it was just how things were back then. So I returned home after three years and took an office job at a local company. That's where I met my husband, and we married when I was twenty-two.

Coincidentally, the local bus company was short-staffed and offered me a position, so I became a bus guide again. This time, I wondered how to make tours interesting when all you could see were fields stretching to the horizon. Due to staff shortages, I had to return to work just two months after having my first son at twenty-three. It was incredibly challenging. Wanting a second child, I went back to my previous office job and had my second son at thirty-two. Both boys grew up to be cheerful kids who loved baseball.

While family life was relatively peaceful, I was diagnosed with kidney disease at thirty-seven. It wasn't something that could be cured just by taking medication. I was hospitalized and put on steroids, and they recommended a tonsillectomy, though it wasn't a standard treatment at the time. Determined to try everything, I went through four hospitalizations and finally had the surgery. My tonsils were apparently in terrible condition, so removing them proved to be the right choice. Fortunately, I managed to avoid dialysis.

Sometimes I couldn't tell if I was just tired or if it was my symptoms. I'd think, *Maybe I'm worn out from watching the kids' baseball games*. I was so anemic I should have been collapsing, but I'd still drive myself to the hospital. It wasn't an illness that could be controlled with medication, and I think my body was gradually sending out warning signals.

That's when INVEL was introduced to me at a hair salon. Initially, I thought it might help with weight loss, but as I learned more, I realized it could help with my illness too. Wanting to preserve my kidney function for as long as possible, I decided to try anything that might help. I started with the mat—after just a thirty-minute nap, my back felt lighter! Experiencing these benefits, I tried various products. At the time, I was busy with raising children, especially with baseball activities, so I didn't regularly visit the salon; I just used the products for myself.

Once my children became more independent, I started working energetically alongside regular employees. Then at fifty, as my kidneys deteriorated further, I faced the decision between dialysis or transplant. Coincidentally, the hospital I'd been attending had only started performing transplants a few years earlier. Thanks to INVEL extending my kidney function, I had the transplant option available to me. But a transplant meant receiving someone else's kidney. I struggled to bring it up with my family. While grappling with this, I suddenly mentioned "transplant," and both my husband and my mother immediately said "yes." I was incredibly thankful. Tests showed my husband's kidney would be suitable.

We were hospitalized together for a month for the transplant. Of course, we had no income during this time. Then INVEL surprised us with a one-million-yen payment. The connections we'd built allowed us to stay in touch with team members even when I was on a bed, and most importantly, they worked with the mindset of "everyone helping everyone." You truly couldn't find this kind of support anywhere else.

It's been eight years since I encountered INVEL. Of course, it hasn't all been smooth sailing. In the beginning, I was juggling multiple jobs, and it was challenging. Since my surgery, I've been focusing exclusively on INVEL. Though, I sometimes doubt myself when working with members, wondering, *What can I really offer everyone?* and feeling perhaps unreliable. But then a leader asked me, "Are you trying to see things from others' perspectives?"

They were right—when I shift my viewpoint, I often realize, "I could do that better." Through interactions with various people, I feel my perspective has broadened. Initially, my dream was simply to afford home renovations. But that's just something money can buy. Now, I want everyone to dream bigger, and beyond that, to achieve spiritual fulfillment and have time for meaningful conversations together. Just like when I was young, I'm enjoying time with friends again. I even performed Shin-buyō at an Invel event! It's rare to find a place where adults can share such genuine laughter together.

Yuko Chiba_08

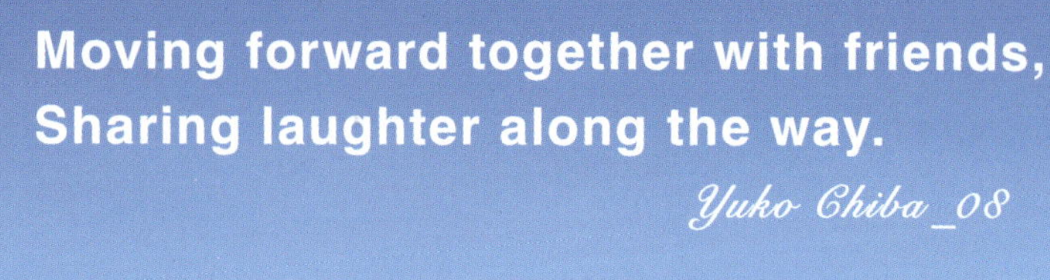
Moving forward together with friends,
Sharing laughter along the way.
Yuko Chiba_08

Atsuko Soma

Hokkaido

You're never truly alone When you have friends you can trust.

I grew up in Makomanai, Sapporo—now famous as a Winter Olympics venue. My father, a civil servant, had a drinking problem, and he would return home after midnight each day. He could be the most wonderful father when sober, but alcohol would transform him completely. Meanwhile, my mother was constantly in and out of hospitals due to her illness. As a result, I became a latchkey kid, letting myself into an empty house after school.

Things weren't easier at school either. I had a strained relationship with my teachers, who seemed to withhold praise no matter how hard I tried or even when I won competitions. Eventually, I lost my motivation and gave up trying. But I couldn't let my sick mother see this side of me. I kept telling myself to stay positive! Sure, it was lonely, but above all, I couldn't bear the thought of causing my mother any more sadness.

Everything changed when I entered high school. I enrolled in a sports-oriented school where no one knew anything about my past; it felt like I could finally spread my wings. I found wonderful classmates and teachers who recognized my efforts, which helped me genuinely believe in trying my best again. I'll never forget the joy of earning a first-level swimming certification, especially since I started as a complete beginner who couldn't swim a single meter.

As high school drew to a close, fate intervened during a visit to relatives in Kyoto. They introduced me to a male colleague, and after spending a few days sightseeing together, he proposed, saying, "Marry me after you graduate." At eighteen, I cheerfully agreed without a second thought. Looking back, I was completely naive about marriage. Though my parents were initially shocked, they approved since he was older and seemed responsible. We married just ten days after my graduation. But our newlywed life in Kyoto wasn't meant to last. Despite his kindness and domestic capabilities, his increasing workload left me alone more often. With no family or friends nearby, I started working and surprisingly found joy in it. This newfound confidence led to a sudden realization: "I want to go back to Sapporo."

Now when I look back, I realize how young I was, and I still feel guilty about what I did to my husband then.

Back in Sapporo, I found my calling in fashion retail. After a decade working at a boutique, I opened my own shop at thirty-three. Nothing brought me more joy than connecting with customers and helping them find the perfect clothes. I truly believed I'd found my life's purpose. But fate had other plans. When I suddenly lost my voice and sought medical attention, I was diagnosed with thyroid cancer that had already spread from my vocal cords to my lymph nodes. The doctors recommended throat surgery, but I was terrified of losing my voice—without it, I couldn't interact with customers, which was everything to me. Life would lose its meaning. I opted for alternative treatments but eventually faced the inevitable need for emergency surgery.

Unable to continue running the boutique, I ventured into restaurant management as a stopgap measure. While trying to keep my boutique afloat, I invested everything in a promising chef and worked tirelessly at the restaurant from dawn till dusk. Just as business was picking up, thanks to the chef's talent, he betrayed me, disappearing with millions of yen in investment. Though I continued with other chefs, my spirit was broken. Even after closing the restaurant, I'm still paying off those loans. It was a harsh lesson: Never again will I take risks on ventures out of my domain; from now on, I'll only trust those who've truly earned it.

During this difficult period, a close friend reached out, suggesting we work together with INVEL. This wasn't actually my first encounter with the company—that happened through a customer's recommendation when I first opened my boutique. I felt obligated to try their compression leggings since a customer suggested it, saying, "They're really good." Surprisingly, just wearing them made me feel better—even my voice, affected by cancer, started returning. I noticed gradual changes in my body. Despite having Raynaud's syndrome, which previously meant I couldn't even enjoy a single soft-serve ice cream in summer, I could now eat two. I got into a routine:

wear them, wash them, and once dry, wear them again. I became devoted to these leggings. However, this was during the period when I was betrayed by the chef, and I was too devastated to continue with anything.

When my friend reached out again, it brought back memories of that earlier time. Then my mother started using their mat, with remarkable results. She had been getting regular injections for fluid retention in her knees due to partial paralysis, but after sleeping on the Invel mat, the fluid retention completely stopped. It's almost unbelievable, but she's walking with such energy now. She's ninety-two, but her skin—both face and back—doesn't look her age at all. I believe we have Invel products to thank for my mother's continued good health.

My commitment to INVEL goes beyond just believing in their products. Throughout my life, I've met all kinds of people, some who drifted away, others who betrayed me. I've always valued trust in relationships. But now, I've come to realize something: It's not just about giving trust, but about having friends who trust each other mutually that brings the greatest joy. That's why I find such pleasure in working alongside the friends I've made through INVEL, supporting and encouraging each other.

My dream for the future is to create a share house. I want to build a welcoming environment where I can reach out to people in need and simply say, "Come over for dinner." Being single without children, I especially want to create a supportive community where we can help each other through life's challenges. Rather than saving money for myself, I want to use it to help others. To achieve this dream, I hope to connect with many more people, and I wish for them to experience better health through Invel's products, even if just a little bit.

Atsuko Soma_09

PIVOT
PARCO
北洋銀行
NORTH PACIFIC BANK
丸井今井

You're never truly alone
When you have friends you can trust.
Atsuko Soma _09

Masayo Kasahara

Saitama

The key to making customers happy Is being healthy yourself.

My gratitude goes to the encounter with INVEL, my husband, and my mother.

I was born and raised in Chichibu City, Saitama, surrounded by abundant nature. My parents ran a barber shop, so I was always playing on the floor of the shop, covered in hair. For as long as I can remember, when the shop got busy and my parents were preoccupied, we had a helper who would look after me and my sister.

As a child, I loved to sing and even participated in a local singing contest. I was comfortable performing in front of others, and in middle school, I joined the chorus club. My parents were too busy to look after their child, so I was enrolled in many lessons—abacus, calligraphy, flower arrangement, piano, and cram school. While I had some kind of lesson almost every day, I was forbidden from participating in sports because my parents reasoned, "Since she's been an active child from a young age, if she starts sports, her studies will suffer."

Finally, after finishing my exams, I got permission to join the *kyudo* (Japanese archery) club in high school. Since kyudo was a rare sport in middle schools, I thought there would not be much difference in skill level among kyudo players. In my third year, when I heard about an upcoming national competition, I made it my goal and worked hard toward it. Remarkably, I was selected to represent Saitama along with two junior students, and we even made it into the newspaper. However, I fell into a slump three days before the main event and ended up being an alternate. Though I felt disappointed, I was comforted by my juniors' warm words: "We made it this far because you were our leader."

Around the same time, I started taking correspondence courses for a hairdressing license. After graduating high school, I spent a year apprenticing at a hair salon in Tokyo and obtained my national hairdressing license. At that time, our family business had expanded from the barber shop to include a beauty salon, but since neither of my parents had a beautician's license, they had to rely on others to run it. Wanting to help, and with my mother's encouragement, I enrolled in a school in Tokyo. I made the three-and-a-half-hour train commute each way, working toward my national beautician's license. It was a prestigious beauty school with over a hundred years of history and strict rules. While the principal was stern, he was also kind enough to let students stay at his home if they were late finishing their self-practice. His daughter was my classmate, and we remain good friends even today.

I got married at twenty-three through an arranged marriage. My husband was a hairdresser and was adopted as a son-in-law. His mother and my father got along wonderfully, and my mother-in-law took a real liking to me. The following year, I gave birth to my first daughter. Life seemed truly blessed.

Everything changed when I was twenty-seven. Shortly after giving birth to my second daughter, I developed a collagen disease. I tried everything—moxibustion, acupuncture, extracts from soft-shelled turtle and viper, massage, and obviously various hospital treatments—but nothing worked, and I became bedridden. I couldn't even breastfeed my baby. To make matters worse, my eldest daughter was hospitalized with acute nephritis. I was also hospitalized for my collagen disease treatment. During this time, my husband and my sister cared for my five-month-old second daughter, allowing me to focus on recovery, and eventually, I regained enough strength to return to work.

Sometime later, our shop's beautician quit, and I had to take over running the beauty salon. I was thirty-five then. This marked my second major crisis; the former beautician had taken all our customers with her. Days passed with no customers coming, and I was constantly anxious, but I decided to turn this crisis into an opportunity by taking training in Tokyo. I went to learn new techniques and trends, attending weekly sessions not just for cuts and perms, but also for makeup and styling. It took three years to rebuild our customer base. Once the business got back on track, I spent my days tricking my body with massages, nutritional supplements, and other methods to get the job done. Then, at forty-nine, I was introduced to a good nutritional supplement and my condition improved. This became my first experience with network marketing.

As the saying goes, bad things come in threes—and sure enough, another crisis struck when I was sixty. My collagen disease returned, and my mother developed a trigger finger. I reached out to Mr. Shioya, the chiropractor who had helped me earlier, which led to my introduction to INVEL. His wife brought me a product, suggesting, "There's something that relieves pain just by wearing it. Why don't you try it?" My mother put on the gloves and almost immediately said, "The pain is gone." When I tried the product myself, I forgot about my body pain and found myself standing up without even thinking about it, amazing everyone present.

My mother thought Invel products were essential to me and purchased quite a lot of them for my personal use. That's when I decided to start the Invel business with Mr. Shioya's wife. We worked as a team for three years. However, just as she reached platinum title, her health failed, and she passed away. This was in 2012. It was such a shock that I couldn't continue my activities, and I distanced myself from Mr. Shioya because we would just end up crying if we talked.

About five years passed before I suddenly received a call from Mr. Shioya. He was organizing his wife's belongings and found a notebook where he saw her written objective, "I want to advance my title to Brazilian." He asked me to help him fulfill her wishes in her place. My mother and I were moved by Mr. Shioya's passionate dedication, and determined to regain our business activity, we threw ourselves into working toward that goal.

INVEL is truly a remarkable product. When I had femur fracture surgery at age seventy, I experienced a level of comfort I'd never felt so grateful for during such a procedure. Four patients had surgery on the same day, but while the other three were struggling with fevers, insufficient pain relief, and general discomfort, I slept soundly through the night, thanks to the Invel futon and mat. Later, the head nurse came to my room asking to learn more about the mat. After that, more and more nurses started buying mats—nine of them in total! It makes sense that the nurses, who work in a hospital and see health issues every day, would recognize the value of these products. Since then, my mother and I worked together, with the support of Ms. Takei, Ms. Nakayama, and many more. My mother advanced her title to an INVEList at the age of ninety-three. I am truly grateful to all the members. My mother, who loved Invel products until the very end, passed away peacefully at the age of ninety-five, surrounded by many family members. I have inherited the business from her, and I am now active as an INVEList. I am so grateful.

I believe many people start experiencing various health issues once they pass seventy. Medical care costs a lot these days. I want to share the benefits of INVEL with more people and help them maintain their health. Since developing collagen disease, from a time when I had neither dreams nor hopes, I've been able to bring joy to my customers as a beautician—something only possible because of my restored health. I'm truly grateful to INVEL for this. My gratitude goes to my husband and my mother.

Masayo Kasahara_10

The key to making customers happy
Is being healthy yourself.

Mayumi Yamaguchi

Gunma

I used to think I wouldn't live to see fifty.

When I was in fourth grade, my father's job transferred us from Saitama to Gunma. I really didn't want to move and even said silly things like, "I'll just stay here by myself!" But the kids at my new school were so kind and welcoming. I quickly made friends and felt right at home.

When I started junior high, I joined the gymnastics club because of my friends. I've always loved being active, and I was pretty flexible, so gymnastics was a good fit for me. I trained really hard and even competed in the prefectural tournament! But all that intense training took a toll on my body. By the time I graduated from junior high, I had developed a bunion and even had a small fracture in my spine. I think it was from pushing myself too hard during my growth spurt.

That's why I was determined to join a different club when I started high school . . . but I ended up joining the gymnastics club again! I just couldn't say no to my friends. Luckily, it wasn't as intense as junior high, so I was able to have fun with it. But I always had pain in my lower back. There were days when it hurt so much that I couldn't even walk, and my dad often had to drive me to school.

After graduating high school, I went to vocational school and became a nursery teacher. I loved children. However, I wasn't very good at interacting with parents; my heart would pound every time during parent-teacher meetings. I met my current husband shortly after graduating high school. He came as a patient to the osteopathic clinic where I was working part-time, and when I was twenty-one, he confessed his feelings. We got married at twenty-seven.

Although I had hallux valgus (bunions) and lower back pain from gymnastics, looking back, I was still quite healthy then. The first crisis came after I gave birth to my first son prematurely. While driving, a car suddenly crashed into me from the side. I twisted my body to protect my son, and at that moment, combined with the impact of the accident, my spine was dislocated. And the crises continued.

I was blessed with a second child, but my daughter had gastroesophageal reflux disease. Literally, even if she drank breast milk, it would reflux, and the milk would come out of her eyes and nose. So, I couldn't lay her down sideways, and even at night, I would lean against the wall and hold her all night. While my back was screaming in pain, during those years when my children were one and two, I spent each day just praying for them to grow up healthy and safe.

Perhaps those prayers were answered, as my daughter's symptoms gradually improved. However, my back pain continued to worsen. At thirty-five, when my daughter turned two, I decided to seek proper treatment once again. By then, the pain had spread beyond my back to my knees and neck, and I would often be the one crawling around the house, not my children. Even taking my son to soccer practice was incredibly challenging for my back. My husband sometimes coached my son's team, so I couldn't ask him to handle the transport. I carried ice packs everywhere I went, using cooling agents on my neck and back. Unable to lie down at night, I slept sitting up. For 365 days, my routine began with morning visits to the chiropractor. I tried various therapeutic devices and any treatment available, but each day felt like mere survival.

The turning point came about three years and five months ago when a fellow mom lent me an Invel blanket, insisting, "This will definitely help your body!" Upon trying it, I could immediately feel my body responding. The most painful areas became intensely warm, and I thought right away, *This might actually work.*

Later, the same friend encouraged me to try the dome, but I was hesitant. Even the slight jolt of braking would cause severe back pain, and I couldn't be in a car driven by someone else. I didn't think I could endure the hour-long drive to the salon. Plus, I'd heard I had to lie down in the dome. By this point, I had also developed hyperventilation symptoms in addition to my full-body pain. I honestly began thinking I wouldn't live to see fifty. Finally, I gathered my courage and drove myself to the salon with the dome.

I entered with bent legs at first, but in the final ten minutes, I decided to try stretching them out, and to my amazement, I could stretch legs that I hadn't been able to before! That very day, I purchased a set, including a mat, quilt, and wearable products, and began using Invel products for my whole body except when bathing. While it hasn't eliminated all the pain, of course, it has given me back the sensation of being able to move my body, something I hadn't experienced in decades.

Now, besides managing childcare and housework, I've returned to working part-time as a childcare worker. I can sit in a chair and even go for short jogs. While these might seem like ordinary movements to most people, since I had been living without being able to do them, my friends were amazed at my transformation. Even my regular chiropractor was surprised, saying, "Wow, how have you done that?" But you know who's most amazed? My two children.

Because of my full-body pain, I had never been able to take them on trips or even out to eat. They're overjoyed now. As for me, I feel like I've been given a second chance at life. I'm excited, thinking, *What should I do with my life from here?* Moving forward, I want to share this joy and these benefits with others who are suffering similarly. I've already brought both my mother and mother-in-law to the salon, and I tell people I meet at the chiropractor about INVEL if they show interest.

Now that I can move my body, it's not just physical improvement—my spirit is energized, too, and I keep finding more things I want to do. Thanks to discovering INVEL, I've been given another chance to truly live my life.

Mayumi Yamaguchi_11

I used to think
I wouldn't live to see fifty.

Mayumi Yamaguchi_11

Yuko Yamazaki

Niigata

In my life, heaven and hell Arrived simultaneously.

I was born the eldest of three siblings, to a father who worked for the National Railways and a mother who was a telephone switchboard operator. Both parents were incredibly kind to me—my father even built a bed for my cherished doll, while my mother sewed bedding for it. They were both wonderful parents, and we truly lived peaceful days.

This happiness took a dramatic turn when I was in my second year of middle school. During morning radio exercises, I suddenly realized that something was wrong; I couldn't move my leg. After a thorough examination at a university hospital, I was diagnosed with left femur deformity and had to undergo surgery following a lengthy hospitalization. I couldn't even participate in school trips. Using crutches after leaving the hospital was particularly difficult for me during adolescence. But my father would take me to school by motorcycle every morning, and on the way home, my good friends would all help carry my bag. I truly experienced the kindness of people and the value of friendship.

After middle school, I enrolled in a dressmaking school. While I couldn't move my leg well, I had full use of my hands, likely inheriting the manual dexterity from my grandmother and mother. By graduation, I had become so proficient that teachers suggested I become an instructor. Looking back, those three years were truly enjoyable.

After graduating, I found work as a dressmaker at a local Japanese & Western-mixed clothing store. At twenty-four, through an introduction from a senior colleague, I met my future husband. My first impression was that he seemed intimidating, but I was won over by his dependable nature and a firm handshake, and we decided to marry before long. We were then blessed with children—a son and a daughter—and the years passed peacefully.

In my fifty-first year, heaven and hell arrived in my life. I needed a second surgery for my left femur condition, which had been troubling me since middle school. But that was manageable. The real joy came when our eldest son and his wife blessed us with our first grandchild. We celebrated New Year's together—three generations sharing laughter and stories.

However, the very next day, my husband, who was still actively working, was involved in a tragic traffic accident that left him with a brain injury. Though he survived, he was completely immobilized. It was heartbreaking to see him in this state, especially since he had always been such an active person. Meanwhile, I was struggling with my own recovery, moving around on crutches. After about six months, my husband was discharged, but he was confined to a wheelchair, casting a dark shadow over our family's life.

Seven years passed with my husband showing gradual improvement, though he still couldn't walk properly. That's when we learned about INVEL through an acquaintance. Hoping it might help, I purchased some products for him. Remarkably, when he wore them, his condition improved significantly. When he first started walking independently, I could hardly believe my eyes. Since then, he's become inseparable from his Invel products—he even insists on having a spare pair of pants ready when I need to wash them! When INVEL later released a mat, he immediately wanted that too. Before I knew it, he had become quite the ambassador for their belts and necklaces.

The change was remarkable. My husband returned to his old self, joking around and taking pride in his appearance again. He became even more enthusiastic about INVEL than I was, sometimes skipping daycare to attend seminars. But sadly, misfortune struck again. He needed surgery for an irregular heartbeat, but there was a medical error. His last words to me were about buying a cake for his birthday the next day. Our simple exchange of "I understand" became our final conversation. Our ten-year-old grandson kept asking, "Aren't hospitals supposed to help people? Why did

Grandpa die in the hospital?" That same grandson, interestingly enough, is now a nurse. It feels like everything has come full circle.

Let me share one last thing about my husband. Although his story had a tragic ending, discovering Invel products brought such brightness to his final years. Their positive impact spread to me as well, and we often shared smiles, saying, "Meeting INVEL has made our lives bloom." That's why, at his funeral, instead of the traditional white burial garments, we dressed him in black Invel products. We even included his beloved mat in the cremation. Our children and grandchildren now joke, "He must be the first person to enter heaven wearing Invel clothes and lying on an Invel mat." When I think about all the precious memories we created, it brings a small measure of peace to my heart.

When I reflect on my life's journey, I've certainly experienced both joys and sorrows. But now, at this age, I've come to realize that the human heart is what matters most. The kindness we show each other is life's greatest beauty. Your own mindset can brighten each day, and the warmth of family and friends can help you overcome any challenge. Perhaps this is the most important lesson I learned through my experience with INVEL.

Yuko Yamazaki_12

In my life, heaven and hell
Arrived simultaneously.

Yuko Yamazaki_12

Eriko Araki

Gunma

No matter how difficult the situation, It can be changed From this moment forward.

I grew up in a family that ran a textile business. My mother started it, and my father later joined to help run it. As the third of four siblings, I had a lonely childhood; my mother was always busy working with my less-capable sister, and I rarely felt her love. This led me to sometimes act out and disappoint my parents.

In high school, I joined the badminton club and lived in my own world, focused only on sports, and somewhat sheltered from reality. After graduation, I found work at the Kiryu Credit Bank, which is where I met my husband. Our parents were actually acquaintances. My father was particularly fond of my husband and enjoyed his visits. Before we married, my husband and my father would drink together almost every day.

Perhaps as a result, my husband would often hide in his car during work hours at the family business, sleeping off two-day hangovers. Because of this behavior, just three days after our wedding, my mother-in-law confronted me, saying, "What kind of despicable woman are you to turn my son into such a worthless person?" Those words cut deep. It was the most painful experience of my life.

While I had often disappointed my own parents before marriage, now I was causing distress to my in-laws. Deciding this couldn't continue, I resolved to change and began helping with the wooden framework for car cushions in my husband's family business. During the economic downturn, I took on multiple jobs beyond the family business: delivering newspapers in the morning, working at a convenience store, working at a dumpling shop, and even managing a ramen shop at night. I worked tirelessly.

Though it was challenging, I found it incredibly fulfilling and exciting. Perhaps due to my sheltered upbringing, everything felt like a new adventure. I maintained a positive outlook, even during difficult times. I even turned my morning paper route into badminton practice, stepping "left-right" while delivering papers. This dedication actually led to me winning the Kiryu City badminton tournament. Maybe this unstoppable determination came from watching my mother work so hard during my childhood.

That same mother suffered a stroke and passed away when I was around fifty. I had brought her to live with me just a few months before her death, which led to overwhelming guilt. Thoughts that I might have shortened her life haunted me, and I cried every day. Around that time, I also stopped working at my husband's wooden frame shop. During this period of grief, my husband said to me, "From now on, Eriko, just do what makes you happy." He is truly the best husband I could have ever wished for.

Having gained experience massaging acquaintances' shoulders and backs, I decided to enroll in a chiropractic school. There, I learned about Dr. Joseph Murphy's latent consciousness utilization method—essentially, a technique for unlocking one's potential. I immersed myself in the practice, listening to training tapes during every possible moment: while driving, resting, even in the bath. Before long, people naturally began gathering around me, and I found myself with a growing number of devoted followers. The school also sold various products—citric acid supplements, enzymes, and therapeutic devices—which my followers eagerly purchased. I eventually served on several committees and became an instructor, rising to the top position in the school. I was even awarded the "Development Award," the first of its kind in the school's fifty-year history.

My introduction to INVEL came through a chiropractor who had graduated from the same school. What happened next was extraordinary. The day after learning about INVEL, I heard a woman's voice upon waking, saying, "Let's do this together." Though the chiropractor's wife had passed away, I felt that perhaps she was watching over him from above, and this inspired me to take on this new challenge.

My greatest transformation after joining INVEL was realizing that change can begin this very moment. This was put to the test during a seminar in Kyushu when the *Shinkansen* service was halted due to an incident. After hours of waiting, we were transferred to another express train, where most people had to stand. While standing in the crowded train, I received a message from an Invel member. When I described my situation, they advised me to "visualize universal energy flowing in while maintaining a sense of gratitude." Following this guidance brought immediate relief.

As my physical condition improved, I came to understand that with universal energy and gratitude, any situation can be turned around. Since then, through meditation, I've been able to let go of all my anxieties about current situations and frustrations about things not going as planned.

Naturally, working in network marketing comes with daily challenges. People sometimes say unkind things. But these words no longer affect me. While problems still arise, their resolution always leads to better outcomes. Currently, I'm working toward earning the Universe title (the highest and most prestigious title; only three distributors have reached this position in INVEL's twenty-year history). My ultimate dream is to establish a chiropractic school in a developing country using INVEL. I make regular donations to UNICEF, but my real passion is creating fundamental change—to ensure children in impoverished countries don't have to scavenge for food in garbage bins and young girls aren't forced into selling themselves. My ultimate goal is to achieve these changes and, at the end of my life, to be able to look back and think, *It was a life well lived!*

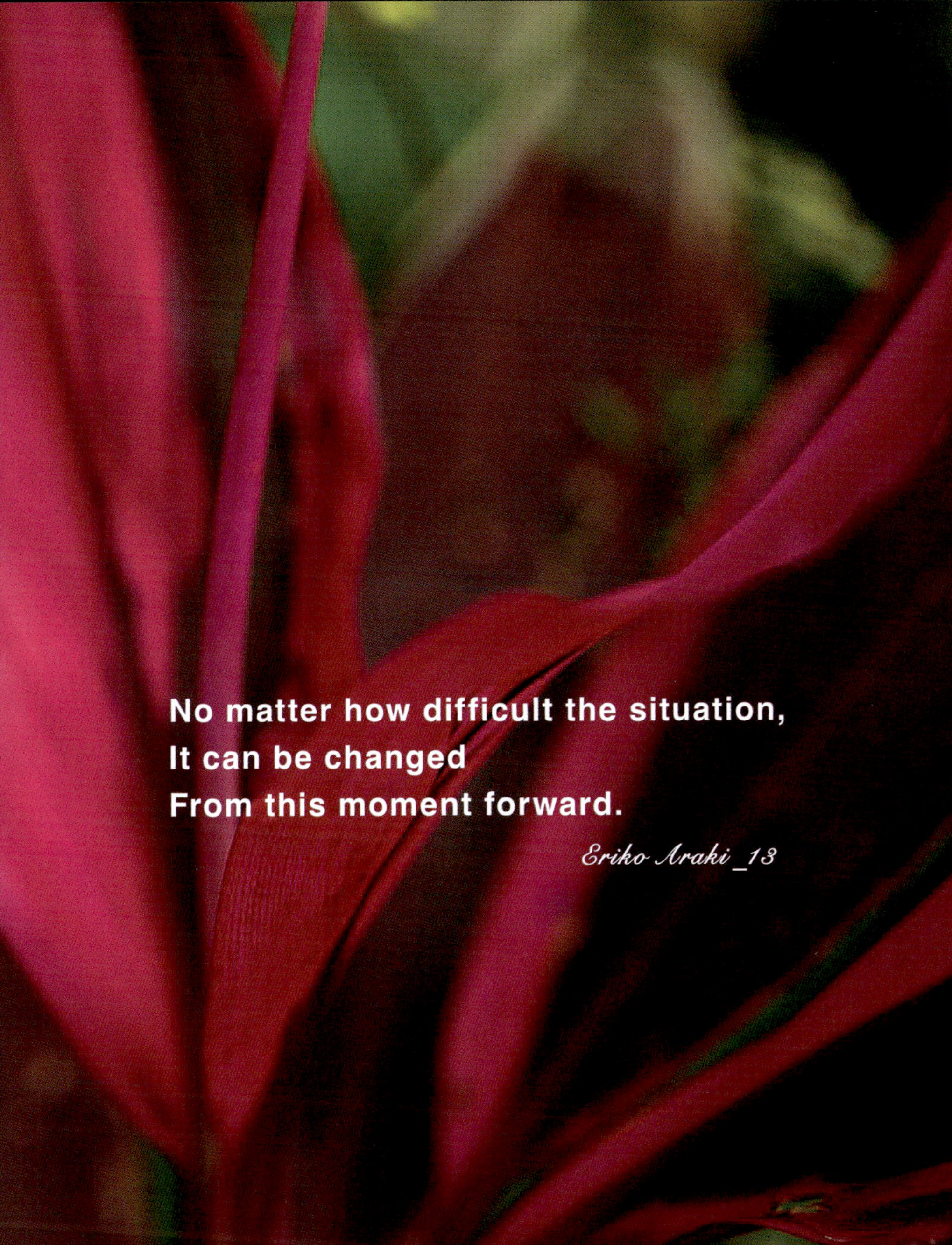
No matter how difficult the situation,
It can be changed
From this moment forward.
Eriko Araki_13

Manami Sako

Saitama

In searching for true health, I discovered my answer.

I believe my life's mission is to share the concepts of "true health," "true beauty," and "true happiness"—perhaps this was my destiny from birth. Born to a newspaper reporter father and a temple maiden mother, I had a difficult start in life.

A complicated forceps delivery left me with a broken left arm, a dislocated joint, and severed nerves. Doctors declared I would never regain movement. But my mother never gave up, taking me to therapeutic massages daily. She raised me with both love and discipline, teaching me everything from piano to proper etiquette. Having an aptitude for mathematics and a fascination with the human body, I dreamed of pursuing medicine from an early age. This led me to pharmacy school, where I thoroughly enjoyed university life, even founding a film drama club where I played the role of a female spy with a rifle.

After graduating, I began working at a dispensing pharmacy and married at twenty-four. Yet I felt unsettled. I hadn't yet found what I should truly dedicate my life to. People would say I might find it after marriage, or perhaps after having children. Hearing such things, I kept searching for my true purpose.

My moment of clarity came at age thirty-six, when I was diagnosed with breast cancer. The doctors recommended surgery, but I made the bold decision to heal myself through alternative means. During this time, my entire family was struggling with health issues: My older child and husband had atopic dermatitis, my younger child suffered from asthma, and my father was dealing with ulcerative colitis. Being a pharmacist, I felt it was my responsibility to help my family overcome these challenges.

I threw myself into research and experimentation, ultimately focusing on six key elements of health: mental well-being, diet, exercise, environment, breathing, and sleep—essentially, restructuring our entire lifestyle. This comprehensive approach became what I call "true health." To share this knowledge, I established a health awareness circle, particularly focusing on teaching children about preventive healthcare before illness strikes.

As a pharmacist who believed in minimizing medication, I began giving lectures about proper medicine use and the importance of nutrition. Then came a pivotal moment. During my volunteer work, I met someone who showed me what they called their "light work" tools, something glowing from their bag. I was instantly captivated. It took me nearly an hour to realize I was looking at what appeared to be black gloves. When I tried to put them on, I experienced an unusual sensation, a tingling that initially made it difficult to touch them. After about thirty minutes, I managed to wear them and was amazed by the experience. I could feel my cells vibrating, my blood flow changing, and all my senses heightening. While the person was surprised by my acute sensitivity to the product, and some readers might be skeptical of this account, this extraordinary experience marked my first encounter with INVEL. I knew immediately that this was more than a coincidence—it was destiny with profound meaning.

I should mention that I was initially very skeptical of network business. Past negative experiences had left me thinking it wasn't aligned with my values. But INVEL was entirely different. The more I researched, the more impressed I became with every aspect: the company, the products, and their system. Learning that they collected clinical data for all their products and that some countries even used them in medical treatment was extraordinary. Their approach was simple, safe, and sustainable.

Moreover, the therapeutic waves benefited not just individuals but entire families and communities. This was a company committed to only releasing products with proven results. After achieving the INVEList title, I was invited to attend a researchers' symposium. While I had already witnessed countless people's health transformations and their joy, hearing the doctors' presentations at this symposium solidified my conviction.

My own experience was equally remarkable. The chronic lower back pain I'd endured for twenty-five years improved, and I noticed changes in my appearance and overall well-being. My biological age seemed to reverse by several years, prompting questions from curious friends. But the most profound moment came when I shared INVEL with a hospitalized friend battling terminal cancer. She told me, "Manami, your mission is to share INVEL with everyone, both those who are ill and those who are well." Five days later, my friend passed away. At that moment, I understood—this truly was my life's mission. That's when I made my unwavering commitment.

When I speak about INVEL now, I explain it this way: We've transformed from rigid robots back into truly *human* beings, with blood flowing to every cell, our bodies finally relaxing. It's crucial to care for ourselves so we don't miss the important signals our bodies and minds send through illness. INVEL, when used properly, helps us become more attuned to these signals.

Beyond just physical health, I believe it can activate dormant abilities and talents that work at the subconscious level during sleep. I've witnessed numerous remarkable examples of this, including professional athletes and musicians experiencing amazing results with INVEL. Through this remarkable technology, I'm dedicated to spreading the message of "true health," "true beauty," and "true happiness" to help everyone achieve their radiant potential.

Finding INVEL has brought me genuine happiness, fulfilled countless dreams, and surrounded me with amazing people who share in this joy. Each day brings new insights and opportunities for growth. For those who wish to stay healthy and active until you are one hundred, enjoying life with friends while continuing to work, INVEL is essential. I'm deeply grateful for this blessing. Together, we'll continue building an ever-brighter future where everyone can thrive.

Manami Sako_14

In searching for true health,
I discovered my answer.

Manami Sako_14

Chieko Takei

Hokkaido

Change your perspective, And life will surely follow!

As one of four siblings—three boys and a girl—I spent my childhood roaming the mountains of Niigata with my brothers. I especially loved playing shop, fascinated by the act of buying and selling. In middle school, I reluctantly played the electronic organ in the brass band, though volleyball, which my mother opposed, was my true passion. When I entered high school, I finally followed my heart and joined the volleyball club. Despite the grueling schedule with breaks only on New Year's, I loved every moment. It was my first taste of freedom.

That yearning for freedom eventually led me to Tokyo. Looking back, I might have done anything, but I chose Tokyo with a heart full of adventure. There, I experienced complete freedom, even living carefree on just 50 yen per week. Eventually, I joined a company as an office worker, got what seemed like a promising marriage, and moved to Sapporo—only to find myself back in a world of constraints.

I had my first son at twenty-nine and my second at thirty-five. It was typical of the times, and my role was clearly defined: handle all childcare and housework, as was expected of women. Living next to my in-laws, I felt suffocated as a daughter-in-law. When the children started elementary school, I began working as a milk delivery person—at least it got me out of the house. This marked the beginning of another chapter in my insane story of freedom.

Obviously, I found joy in it. Each time my collection pouch grew heavier, I felt a thrill reminiscent of my childhood days playing shop. Unlike my previous job in apparel, milk delivery gave me tangible satisfaction, the joy of sales and of truly living. Then I went on to work as a nursing assistant and in funeral services for a mutual aid society. Starting with door-to-door sales was tough; initially, no one would open their doors. But gradually, doors began to open, one after another. It felt like destiny was finally smiling on me as contracts started coming in, and I experienced the deep satisfaction of being fairly compensated for my dedication.

Just as I was finding my stride at work, my husband suddenly passed away. With my younger son still in his third year of middle school and future education expenses looming, I was terrified about managing my salary alone. Searching for direction in this darkness, I attended a lecture by Hiromi Nakano, an impressive woman with a global presence. She mentioned that, "We are connected to the universe," and that struck a deep chord within me.

While the universe typically seems remote and abstract, here was someone who not only seemed deeply connected to it but spoke about it with such a commanding presence that I was captivated. Eager to explore this invisible realm further, I began studying and attending other women's talks. Each new encounter left me more amazed. "We can wish for anything. We were born to find happiness!" she declared.

"What? I'm allowed to be happy?" I realized I had always felt guilty about pursuing my happiness. I had prioritized my duties as a wife and mother, constantly suppressing my own desires. My life had been like endlessly pedaling a bicycle while carrying a heavy burden on my back. But now I understood that it was okay to want things for myself. That day, in an act of bold visualization, I cut out a model's photo, pasted my face over it, and, without questioning whether it was foolish, posted a note on my wall declaring, "Monthly income: 4.5 million yen."

It all started during a phone conversation with my sister-in-law, who mentioned, "A friend seems to have lost weight wearing some spats . . ." When I asked her to get one for me, a salesperson of this company (my future upline) visited me for a product presentation. That was February 2007, my first encounter with INVEL. The effect was immediate—within five minutes of touching the product, my hands were tingling. It could even reduce wrinkles beyond what was normal for my age; I'd never seen anything like it.

I knew instantly this was a product everyone would want, destined for success. I could see the bright future right then! However, I had no interest in network marketing. When asked to help organize a seminar venue, I reluctantly agreed and intentionally invited just three people. Despite the tiny turnout, the presenter came all the way from Tokyo and spoke passionately, even promising to return in two weeks.

I couldn't help but ask why he would invest so much time in someone with no connections or experience in network marketing. His response was enlightening: "INVEL's system can be mastered in just three days, and the products are like gifts from the universe!" This was during a time when I was fascinated by concepts like universal existence, luck, and human potential. His answer resonated deeply!

I realized this was a product humanity needed, completely different from typical network businesses. Knowing I was sharing a company that 99 percent of people would seek, I threw myself into seminar recruitment, mobilizing thirty people in just two weeks. I transformed my life in those two weeks!

The most amazing part? That 4.5-million-yen goal I'd posted on my wall manifested exactly one year later as a deposit in my account! And another 4.5 million the following year. Looking back at that seemingly naive wall posting in my room, I realize that my self-made promise materialized into a miracle before my eyes. Humans truly are remarkable! Anyone can become a magician! My entire perspective has shifted, and I deeply understand now that we are born to be happy.

Change your worldview, and your life will inevitably transform! Walking this path for eighteen years and two months, now entering my nineteenth year, I still approach each day with excitement. Destiny is all about connections, and I'm grateful for every single one.

Chieko Takei_15

Change your perspective,
And life will surely follow!
Chieko Takei_15

Yuko Sato

Aichi

Finding my inner strength and Sharing it with others.

When I was a child, I had to eat my meals while being hit with a bamboo stick—something unthinkable in today's world. Yet my parents' strictness had its reasons. Having lost my brother when he was just two months old, their stern approach came from a place of deep love. In retrospect, rather than abuse, it was perhaps reflective of an era where children were expected to develop resilience.

By the time I entered elementary school, my mother had become our primary provider. My father was frequently hospitalized due to an accident and kidney problems, while my mother worked as a nurse despite having undergone a mastectomy due to breast cancer. I took on the responsibility of caring for my younger siblings: preparing meals and taking my siblings by public transport to see my father in the hospital on holidays. This pattern continued through junior high school, with part-time jobs added during high school. Watching my classmates enjoying their free time sometimes filled me with envy. Reading became my sole escape, offering brief moments of respite. Looking back, I realize these experiences built the resilience that would serve me throughout life.

Post-high school, I juggled nursing school with work. My days were an endless cycle of classes, practical training, report writing, and jobs. The lack of sleep took its toll on both my physical and mental health, leading me to drop out six months before completing the two-year program. Then I quit the job as well, though quitting brought an unexpected sense of liberation. I then found work at a local food manufacturer, but it was during the economic downturn and deflation spiral. The company faced the impossible task of managing rising raw material costs while maintaining competitive pricing, leading to successive layoffs. When my turn came, I quit, thinking, *Why me? I'm only in my first year.*

From there, while receiving unemployment benefits, I looked for work and fortunately found a position at an auto parts manufacturer. That's where I met my husband. My first impression was that he looked young compared to the fact that he is nine years older. After a year or so, he said, "I want to drink miso soup every day."

I casually replied, “Why don’t you make it yourself?” But that turned out to be his marriage proposal!

Our marriage began simply, and at twenty-three, I became pregnant and gave birth. We had another child, and I spent my time raising our two boys. I wanted to instill life skills in my children somehow. My husband was the type who couldn’t do anything around the house. With our eldest, parenting was incredibly difficult. He was constantly moving, running around. Since child leashes weren’t common then, I was desperately trying to prevent accidents. On the other hand, the younger one was quite the opposite, more reserved.

One day, my younger son was diagnosed with suspected developmental issues. Something clicked in my mind, and I asked for an examination for my elder son. Both turned out to have conditions. My eldest was the hyperactive type, diagnosed with ADHD. My younger one was more passive, with delayed speech development, unable to respond to what was said, and prone to tantrums.

While the diagnoses helped us understand their behaviors, the daily challenges remained significant. Memory issues became commonplace, and behavioral problems led to various social conflicts. My days were filled with calls from teachers and making apologies, yet I made a conscious decision to discuss their conditions exclusively with their teachers. I forced myself to recognize that their conditions and the issues they caused were two different things. I thought that their conditions shouldn’t define their future social interactions. My husband struggled to accept their diagnoses, leaving me feeling isolated at times. Although I had to manage their rebellious period, I am proud of how they’ve grown. When they’d call me “damn old lady,” I’d jokingly ask them to repeat it for a video.

Today, my eldest is pursuing a university degree through distance learning, and my younger son is employed—both carving their own paths successfully. They’ve become self-sufficient, even helping with household chores. In this era of online learning, where even Harvard offers remote courses, my eldest chose distance education himself, citing COVID-19 concerns. I’m grateful they developed the resilience that now serves as their foundation for personal growth. After all, true abundance can only come from having your life in order.

After the intense years of child-rearing, I was working in body care and cafés—fields I'd always found interesting—when I encountered INVEL last winter. My first experience with the dome was revelatory; I immediately recognized its uniqueness. The distinctive frequency penetrates deeply, providing warmth to your core. My nursing school background helped me understand its physiological benefits, and I appreciated the simplicity of the treatment, just lying under the dome or wearing the clothing. The timing was particularly meaningful as my mother had recently undergone breast cancer treatment, and she found great comfort in the dome therapy.

One memorable experience was with a body care client who had lower-body paralysis. When I placed an Invel blanket over their paralyzed areas, they experienced warmth—a powerful demonstration of its effectiveness. When my younger son expressed interest in trying it for his back pain, I playfully told him to save up and buy it himself. I'm also noticing its effects on beauty and anti-aging. Since starting to use it, many people have said, "You look prettier. What changed?" You know how medical beauty treatments are trending now? With INVEL, you can achieve results through daily life without surgery. As a body care therapist, I'm eager to promote these beauty benefits, and my current goal is to establish a salon with an Invel dome.

I've heard that INVEL plans to refresh their design and strengthen their beauty line, which could attract a younger demographic. I'm excited about finding my role in this evolution. The prospect of contributing to this growth fills me with anticipation and purpose. I cannot help but look forward to it.

Yuko Sato_16

Finding my inner strength and Sharing it with others.

Yuko Sato_16

Sachie Nakano

Fukuoka

Being mindful of how money exists, Being grateful for how people exist.

Growing up, my father was a teacher and quite the disciplinarian. His strict rules and frequent scolding shaped my early years. Whether it was regular studies or piano lessons, I never missed a day. Coming from Shimonoseki City in Yamaguchi, owning a piano was quite rare back then. Looking back, I realize how much my father invested in my education despite his stern nature. I later attended a private middle school affiliated with a junior college, where I made wonderful friends and created lasting memories.

After graduation, I started my career in office work. Within my second year of working, I met my now-husband and got married. We were blessed with two children—a daughter and a son. When I reached my thirties, as the children became more independent, I established a tutoring school from home. Perhaps inheriting my father's teaching spirit, I felt compelled to contribute to children's education in our community. With my middle school English teaching certification, I began with English lessons and later expanded to mathematics. The conversations with students about their dreams and aspirations were truly precious moments.

I continued teaching for about two decades, until I was fifty. Around that time, I also developed my cooking skills in a very short time. With evening tutoring sessions, I learned to prepare family dinners efficiently beforehand. It may be my pride that I have never fed my family with convenient, ready-cooked stuff. As a dual-income household, we were fortunate to never face financial hardship. We could afford to eat what we enjoyed and buy what we desired. I suppose this comfortable lifestyle eventually caused us punishment.

Our financial troubles began when my husband had to stop working when he was fifty-seven. He retired from his position at a construction company. He became consumed with entertainment, golf, and more entertainment for his clients. Without any prior discussion, he suddenly announced one day, "I'm submitting my resignation." Having lived a blessed life until then, I naively responded, "Okay, we'll manage somehow." But that's when our real struggles began.

Although my husband found new employment, his salary was significantly reduced. We couldn't maintain our previous lifestyle. We had both house and car loans, but no money to pay them. Thoughts of payments consumed me, leading to many sleepless nights. We even had cars for all family members; I realized that we were living beyond our means.

That's when I first learned about proper budgeting. Previously, I hadn't even kept track of what was in our refrigerator, often discovering spoiled food at the back. To begin fixing this, I started cleaning the refrigerator before shopping. I would check what ingredients we had actually used up and only buy the absolute necessities. Through this penny-pinching lifestyle, I learned the true value of money.

I encountered INVEL during these challenging times. I had been involved in other network businesses since my forties, and some friends I met through those introduced me to it. They told me, "This will change your life," and while I was skeptical at first, it really did. Such encounters are truly precious.

Initially, I was impressed by their products. While I was knowledgeable about health foods and supplements due to my interest in health management, I realized that these products were different—simply wearing them was effective, and it felt like a glimpse into the future. I had suffered from chronic shoulder pain and relied on daily headache medication, but when I tried their "card" (a fabric card embedded with INVEL's unique "MIG3" technology, made of bio ceramics) on the affected area, the pain disappeared faster than with medicine! It was extraordinary! Everything fell into place after that.

At that time, we were truly broke. We couldn't even secure a loan from banks or credit card companies for the initial sign-up fee of 250,000 yen. Swallowing my pride, I had to ask my daughter for help. Though I managed to become a distributor, I couldn't even afford transportation costs or refreshments for business consultations. I resorted to hosting people at home, serving them meals; cooking was something I was confident about, at least. But then our electricity was cut off, and I couldn't even invite people over anymore. Ironically, the leaders used to introduce me as "Ms. Nakano in grinding poverty."

After a year of trial and error, I achieved an annual income of 1.5 million yen and could finally repay my daughter. But this was just the beginning. I knew there must be others like me struggling with both health and finances. I began to realize that INVEL could help improve both people's physical and financial well-being. There's still so much growth potential, and the leaders' guidance was invaluable. Even when I was discouraged by canceled contracts, they helped me work through solutions. They would even argue with headquarters to protect me. They're still working alongside me today—such wonderful people who would go to such lengths for others.

It's been thirteen years since joining INVEL. Thanks to the support of those around me, my income has increased steadily. My husband worked until he was sixty-eight, and now he says, "We're doing alright now, thanks to Mom." Our children have their own families now, but they often invite us over, saying, "Let's enjoy a nice meal together." I can tell they're trying to be fed with my earnings; it makes me happy, though.

There was a time when I caused them to worry in their daily lives, so now I'm working hard to redeem myself. Through it all, even in difficult times, our family bonds have remained strong. Back then, my husband and I would joke, "Even in poverty, at least we're alive!" Looking back, I guess we were cheerfully poor.

Looking ahead, my dream is to double my current annual income. And just as others helped me, I want to help as many people as possible. I'm just a chatty grandmother who enjoys health management and helping others. Now I realize it was actually fortunate that I hit rock bottom while I still had the energy to bounce back. Those difficult times taught me to truly appreciate the value of money. They also helped me rediscover the importance of human relationships. And now, at this age, I've developed such a positive outlook on life. Life really does have a way of transforming itself.

Sachie Nakano_17

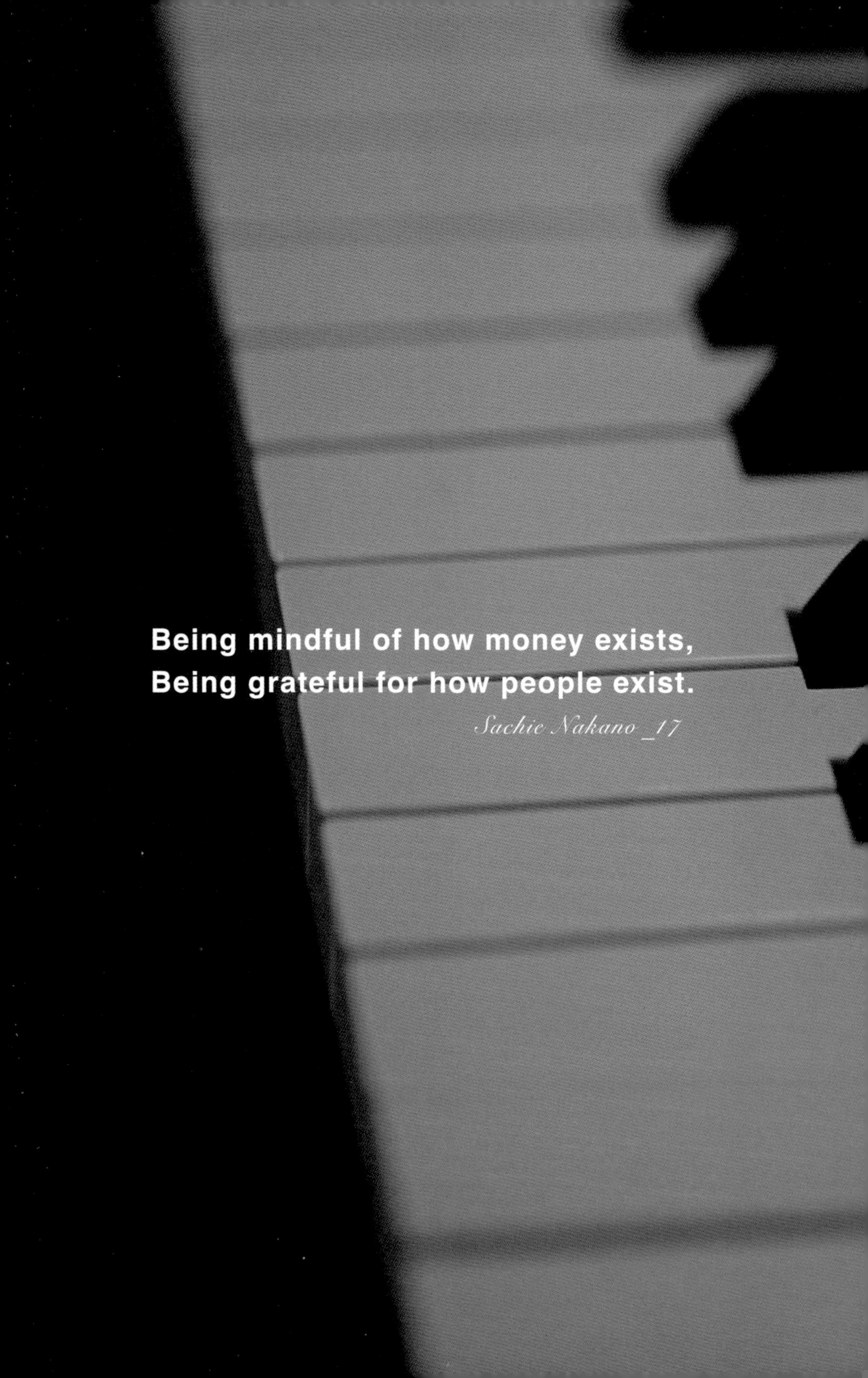

Being mindful of how money exists,
Being grateful for how people exist.

Sachie Nakano _17

Tokiko Kajiki

Saitama

I lived like a restless bug. And I will continue to live this way.

My father's career as a national civil servant meant frequent transfers, and our family moved with each posting. Though we mostly stayed within Kagoshima, I remember experiencing bullying in elementary school for being the new transfer student. Later, in middle school, I transferred from a rural school to one in the city, where I struggled with a significant gap in academic progress.

Despite these challenges, I was particularly favored by my PE teacher, who chose me to represent students at morning assemblies and selected me for relay races even though I wasn't especially fast. Similarly, the drama club teacher took notice of me, leading to my participation in drama competitions. Looking back, I might have been quite noticeable at school.

During high school, I immersed myself in dance and drama. I was particularly inspired by a newly appointed female PE teacher and began studying to enter Nagasaki University of Physical Education, her alma mater. However, after casually taking and passing a company entrance exam during summer break—though I couldn't actually work there due to my father's transfer—I lost all motivation to study and abandoned my university plans. My mother was furious, saying, "What's your problem? Do you get bored easily, or do you just like the beginnings of things? You're like a grasshopper!" Indeed, I was the type to dive enthusiastically into new things but quickly lose interest. Looking back now, I think there was always a curious and restless bug inside my heart.

After high school, I didn't last long at the office job I got through my father's connections. The restless bug emerged again, and I wrote to my uncle in Tokyo and headed to the capital. I found myself on the top floor of the San-Ai building in Ginza, taking in Tokyo's vibrant atmosphere, and seriously contemplating, *How can I work in a place like this?* Eventually, fate led me to a position at Shiseido Central Sales.

It was around this time that I met my current husband—or rather, reconnected with him, as we had been high school classmates. We started dating in Tokyo, but my restless bug surfaced again. After talking with an employee who had returned from an overseas assignment with Shiseido, I was filled with a strong desire to go abroad myself. To improve my chances, even slightly, I requested a transfer to the Kagoshima Sales office, where there was less competition. Though my husband was perplexed by this decision, he faithfully wrote to me throughout my three years in Kagoshima. When I was twenty-five, with a cardboard box full of his letters, we finally got married. During our wedding, I made him promise, "Don't remain just a salaryman forever; start your own business someday." From then on, I think my husband also got caught up in my adventures with the restless bug.

Of course, not all ventures succeed. When I was thirty-two and our first child was born, my husband launched a real estate business while I started selling music tapes, capitalizing on the karaoke boom. Though both businesses started smoothly, everything changed when the economic bubble burst. My husband's real estate venture ground to a halt, and we suddenly found ourselves drowning in debt. Those days are almost a blur now; we were just desperately trying to survive day by day.

I also learned how relationships change when money becomes scarce. I couldn't even genuinely feel happy for friends' weddings or children's births, finding myself thinking, *Why celebrate at such a difficult time?* I was ashamed of those feelings. As people's attitudes around us changed, I realized we had lost not just our finances but our social connections too. Looking back, perhaps losing everything was better than having something left halfway—it allowed us to see our path forward clearly.

Since regular employment wouldn't be enough to handle our substantial debt, we ventured into network business. The first thing I learned in network business was that if you don't recruit, the group won't grow. In my second network business venture, I met Ms. Oe, who would later introduce me to INVEL, and my life took a dramatic turn. The impact Ms. Oe had on my life is too profound to fully express here. Truly, meeting Ms. Oe and discovering INVEL transformed my life completely.

When I think about how I overcame life's challenges, to be honest, I can't quite remember exactly how I managed to pull through. But I do clearly remember finding hope after encountering INVEL. I've learned that it's crucial to move forward with hope rather than being paralyzed by worries. Now, I'm financially secure and can pursue whatever I set my mind to. I can even afford to tip taxi drivers generously as a gesture of gratitude. At this stage in my life, I feel I've finally achieved true freedom.

Death comes to everyone eventually. But shouldn't we live by pursuing something meaningful regardless? I want to continue living according to my beliefs, just as I have until now. Now that I've built a foundation with INVEL, my restless bug has recently started stirring again. And you know what? I'm ready to go anywhere to help others.

Tokiko Kajiki_18

I lived like a restless bug.
And I will continue to live this way.

Tokiko Kajiki_18

Mayumi Yoshida

Fukuoka

Every moment with others Is irreplaceable, For it will never come again.

My mother exists only in the void of my memory. She was hospitalized when I was about two and passed away before I started elementary school. Afterward, my father raised my brother and me alone—though that's not quite accurate, as my grandmother was always there supporting us. Perhaps because of this home environment, I became highly attuned to adults' emotions, often putting on a cheerful face when I sensed it was needed.

School was challenging. I found it difficult when teachers enforced group activities, expecting children to act in prescribed ways. After somehow making it through each school day, I'd return home to find Grandmother had prepared homemade treats like steamed bread and *zenzai*. After eating, I'd stay quietly at home, not going out. Throughout high school, she made my lunch every day. It would take me some time to truly appreciate the value of these loving gestures.

After high school, I happened to find a job offer at a beauty salon where I began working. I enrolled in beauty school to get certified, but I struggled with workplace relationships and quit. My father was furious when I made this decision unilaterally. After a heated argument, I ran away from home. Yet even afterward, being naturally timid, I couldn't maintain steady employment. I drifted between part-time jobs every few months, barely making enough to eat, with only my aesthetic salon work lasting about four years.

While aimlessly moving through my twenties, I received news of my grandmother's hospitalization. I hadn't seen her since leaving home. Feeling remorseful, I borrowed a friend's car and began visiting her. But she grew frailer by the day, losing her ability to speak. One day, she expressed a desire for nectar juice, that pink juice she had always loved. But her condition wouldn't allow it. The helplessness of not being able to fulfill even this simple wish crushed me. Regret overwhelmed me—why hadn't I been more responsible? Why hadn't I spent more time with her? After her passing, I gradually distanced myself from my family home. I couldn't bear to see her empty room.

Around age twenty-eight, I was running a small aesthetic salon from a rented room. While keeping busy with work, I was also trying to cope with the grief of losing my grandmother. Despite working constantly, I was barely making ends meet, surviving on part-time jobs recommended by acquaintances and clients. During a visit to the employment office, I came across an aesthetic position opening and went for an interview. There, I met the person who would later become the salon owner who introduced me to INVEL. My first impression was of an elegantly stylish person holding a toy poodle.

After performing a trial treatment as part of the interview, she asked if I could start the next day, adding, "I'm often out during the day. Would you mind watching this dog at the salon?" Actually, I hate animals a lot. But I eagerly agreed, hoping to secure the position. True to their word, the owner was rarely present. Despite keeping proper books, the salon's income alone wasn't sustainable. On days when there were seminars elsewhere, all the customers would attend those instead, leaving the salon empty. This owner was said to earn a billion yen.

During one such empty day, I mustered the courage to ask for time off, and she invited me to join the seminar instead. Though I initially declined, my boyfriend at the time encouraged me to go, giving me transportation money and saying, "Go meet someone who makes a billion yen!" At the seminar, I gathered my courage and asked, "How can someone earn a billion yen?"

She replied, "Just decide your target amount and show the newspaper article to the people around you." That's when I thought maybe I could do it too and began my journey with INVEL, putting in my utmost effort.

Starting a new challenge at thirty-one, I was young for an Invel member, and as someone who had been drifting through life, I was completely incompetent. I was constantly being pushed with comments like, "Why can't you understand something so simple?" I was completely inconsiderate of others' feelings and situations. When the owner tried to give me concerned advice, I would defiantly shout, "I can't do that!" slam my desk, and storm out. But this time, I was determined not to give up and to challenge myself for the title. However, having isolated myself with smartphone games and avoiding human contact, I had no network of connections. I didn't even know who to turn to for advice. So I reached out repeatedly to the one person whose contact information I had from my previous part-time job, and my father.

These two people became my support system. Eventually, I managed to achieve my first title. I finally realized how many people had helped me throughout my life. I also became aware that I had always been demanding things while refusing to accept others. INVEL taught me these valuable lessons. As I changed, my relationship with my father changed as well. Now we're both Invel enthusiasts—father and daughter. Looking back, I understand that every interaction with others is precious and irreplaceable, and time once passed never returns. I've come this far supported by many people, surrounded by their warmth and care. And I'll continue moving forward on this path.

Mayumi Yoshida_19

Every moment with others
Is irreplaceable,
For it will never come again.

Mayumi Yoshida_19

Junko Takao

Nagasaki

My experience in America has Shaped the foundation of my life, And I aspire to expand Internationally in the future.

I grew up in Sasebo City, Nagasaki, where I spent my school years. In my youth, everyone used to say, "Junko is destined for the Olympics," because of my exceptional athletic abilities, particularly in running.

I excelled in various sports, and during middle school, I participated in track and field, volleyball, and tennis. I competed in three combined track and field events, winning both city and prefectural championships. In tennis, I was part of a championship-winning team at the national interschool competition. Despite pursuing both academics and athletics, I failed my entrance exams for universities in Tokyo.

Rather than returning home defeated, I pivoted my strategy to move to Tokyo and applied to beauty school. Though I missed the application deadline, I spoke directly with the administration director, received special permission to enroll, and returned home. My family ran a well-established kimono school in Kyushu. To gain my parents' support, I promised to obtain a national beauty qualification, which required studies in Tokyo.

While at school, choosing my internship placement, I discovered a book my mother treasured—*The Beauty of Kimono* by Isoi Hayami. Deeply moved by this work, I wrote to him, hoping to study under his guidance, and I eventually met him in Kamakura. I can still picture his dark green hat and coat. Through his introduction, I secured a year-long practical training position at a beauty salon in Yokohama. Though the training was rigorous, I now recognize how valuable that discipline was for my personal growth. After obtaining my national qualification and completing an additional year of apprenticeship, I began planning my next career move.

Before returning home, I made plans to study in America. Though my mother opposed the idea, my father supported me, telling her, "A woman would be restricted to seek her wish once she would get married," and helped convince her. After a two-week journey on a cargo ship, I arrived in San Francisco. Through a friend's brother's introduction, I enrolled in California's largest beauty education institution, Marinello Beauty School, where I began an entirely new chapter of my life. In America, I discovered that many people prefer beauty salons to schools, and students receive tips from satisfied customers; it was an eye-opening experience. This American journey truly became the foundation of who I am today.

However, after about six months of intense work, I experienced mental burnout. While my skills were quickly recognized and I was placed in the top class, this created unexpected pressure. When I could neither create nor eat properly and was considering returning to Japan, I thought, *If I'm going back, I should see America first.* With just a backpack, I spent a month traveling by Greyhound bus through Arizona, Canada, New York, Florida, Dallas, Houston, Washington, DC, and more. Despite New York's dangerous reputation, I planned to just pass through but ended up staying a week, fascinated by the city. I visited the World Trade Center during its construction, and by chance, met an owner on the 98th floor who gave me a tour—now a precious memory, especially since 2001.

These interactions with locals helped restore my spirit. One month wasn't enough, so I extended my stay, traveling until my funds ran out. By the end, I had just five cents to my name and, unfortunately, encountered a hurricane. I found shelter in a church and stayed at a monastery for three days, kindness I'll never forget. This period gave me much to reflect on: the support I received from strangers during difficult times and my parents who sent money when the exchange rate was 360 yen to the dollar. These experiences became my foundation for life, teaching me the importance of self-control, independence, and maintaining optimism even in challenging situations. This resilience was built through my training, and through these experiences, I developed a deeper understanding of human suffering.

I spent two years in America before returning home due to my mother's illness. While continuing to help with our family business, I developed my own unique kimono style, leading specialized kimono classes and teaching new ways to appreciate traditional dress. I also organized kimono shows twice yearly—still a rarity at that time. The international kimono show in Washington, DC, was particularly enlightening. My career was progressing steadily when I developed painful symptoms in my hands from handling textile tools. This was in 2008. Though hospital visits yielded no diagnosis, a scientist in Fukushima introduced me to Invel gloves, explaining their use in Brazil for treating tendinitis and rheumatism patients. This was my first encounter with INVEL.

Despite my initial skepticism, I was amazed when the pain vanished after just three days of use. While my mother was initially indifferent to my discovery, she became deeply interested once she experienced the product herself and understood INVEL's business model. Recognizing the challenges of sustaining a business solely through kimono, she became even more enthusiastic than me about expanding INVEL's presence, saying, "This is fascinating; we need to promote this as quickly as possible." Tragically, soon after we began working with INVEL, my mother was diagnosed with cancer and given just two months to live. She passed away at eighty-four.

During her final two months, my mother continued using Invel products and remained passionately involved in Invel activities. She seemed driven by a mission to share INVEL's benefits with as many people as possible. Even a week before her passing, she was calling acquaintances, insisting, "I can't die without telling you about this." Witnessing my mother's determination until the very end, I've made an unwavering commitment to carry her mission forward.

I'm fortunate to have a husband who understands and supports my ambitions. We met when I was twenty-seven and married just four months later. He firmly believes that "talented women should be active contributors to society," which has allowed me to pursue both my kimono work and Invel activities freely. We have three daughters, all of whom understand and appreciate INVEL's value. We're grateful to live as an Invel family every day. What makes INVEL exceptional is its all-around excellence—whether in products, business models, or future potential. I envision INVEL's influence expanding to embrace the entire globe, ultimately contributing to world peace. I'm truly excited about our future international expansion.

Moving forward, I remain committed to sharing INVEL's value with as many people as possible, spreading our message that "INVEL is the light of hope" with both love and passion.

Junko Takao_20

**My experience in America has
Shaped the foundation of my life,
And I aspire to expand
Internationally in the future.**

Yuki Ogura

Fukuoka

The strength to overcome hardship Comes from childhood memories and An unwavering belief in the future.

I was born in Yame City, Fukuoka. As the youngest of three siblings, with significant age gaps between my sister and brother, I received abundant affection from my parents. I don't recall my father ever scolding me harshly.

I was a small and sickly child, which kept my mother constantly worried. I still remember how she would bring hot milk to my bedside whenever I called for her in the morning. My childhood was filled with love and carefree days. When I began playing basketball in middle school, I experienced a sudden growth spurt. Though I continued growing until I was twenty, causing my mother concern, I eventually developed into a healthy young woman standing five and a half feet tall.

Our family had maintained a traditional lantern-making business since my grandfather's time, specializing in *bon chochin* lanterns—decorative pieces for Buddhist altars that were a specialty of Yame. The period before the bon festival was particularly busy, and I often helped out. However, sales gradually declined, and I remember overhearing my parents arguing about finances.

Once in elementary school, when I asked my mother for field trip pocket money, she gave me a 100-yen bill she had carefully saved; this was during the era when 100-yen coins were already significant. That's when it hit me: "Our family is struggling financially."

During my high school years, the business went bankrupt. My mother then took a job as a hospital assistant and caregiver to make ends meet. My father, unable to let go of the business, never sought outside employment. Yet even during these difficult times, I maintained an inexplicable, deep-seated belief that my future would be successful. Following my mother's guidance, I enrolled in a high school where I could earn a nursing license. She must have wanted to ensure I would have a stable profession.

After high school, I continued my education at a nursing college, where I successfully obtained my registered nurse qualification. I then began working at a general hospital in Fukuoka. With an interest in international experience, I worked for about two years before spending a month on a homestay in America. Though brief, this period was incredibly meaningful, offering many new experiences and becoming a source of personal growth. I then moved to Tokyo, where my brother lived and worked at a plastic surgery clinic with a bright atmosphere and a positive work environment. After two fulfilling years in Tokyo, I returned to Fukuoka at age twenty-four.

Back home, I resumed hospital work, and within months, met my future husband. Learning about his experience as a youth volunteer in South America captured my interest; I felt that sharing life with someone with a global perspective might expand my own horizons. We married when I was twenty-five, marking a significant turning point in my life. Having experienced family discord in my childhood home, I was determined to create a happy family of my own. My husband, being older, was knowledgeable and kind, someone I could truly respect and admire.

My career then evolved from nursing to public health nursing. When I mentioned my long-standing interest in public health to my husband, he encouraged me to pursue further studies. At twenty-seven, I passed the civil service exam and enrolled in school. Shortly after, I discovered I was pregnant with my first child. Though I struggled with the decision to continue my studies, my due date coincidentally fell during summer break, and the school was remarkably supportive. I attended classes throughout my pregnancy, gave birth during the summer break as planned, and returned to studying just one week after delivery. Within three weeks, I was back at school and in practical training.

My mother helped with childcare during the day, and my husband's support enabled me to maintain my study schedule. I successfully obtained my public health nurse qualification within a year—the most challenging endeavor of my life thus far. The following year, I began my second career as a school nurse teacher at a combined junior and senior high school.

While I'm typically quite influenced by my partner, my introduction to INVEL took a unique path. Though my husband was already involved, I initially showed little interest. When he approached me one day, saying, "I'd like you to hear about this," I was taken aback, as he had never before discussed his work with me. Seeing his enthusiasm, I decided to support him by registering. Later, learning about his financial success with INVEL, I became motivated to venture into the business myself.

The beginning was challenging. Network marketing carried negative connotations in my social circle, leading to frequent rejections. Despite doing nothing wrong, I often felt hurt by people's angry reactions and sometimes fell into depression. However, a fellow mother who had joined told me, "This is incredibly fulfilling," and encouraged me, saying, "Let's persist together until the end." These words shifted my perspective, helping me realize that critics simply hadn't found their edge yet.

I harbor one significant dream. Having achieved financial stability through INVEL, I want to give back to children in my community. In today's Japan, the wealth gap is striking—some children lack proper meals, while others face disparities in access to entertainment and educational experiences. I aim to create a space that provides both nourishment and enjoyment, hoping to build lasting positive memories for these children.

During my nursing studies, one phrase left an indelible impression: WHO's definition of health as "a state of complete physical, mental, and social well-being." This comprehensive definition has stayed with me, and I believe INVEL can help achieve this vision of health. Moving forward, I'm committed to dedicating my life to helping not just myself, but many others in my community achieve better health through INVEL.

Yuki Ogura_21

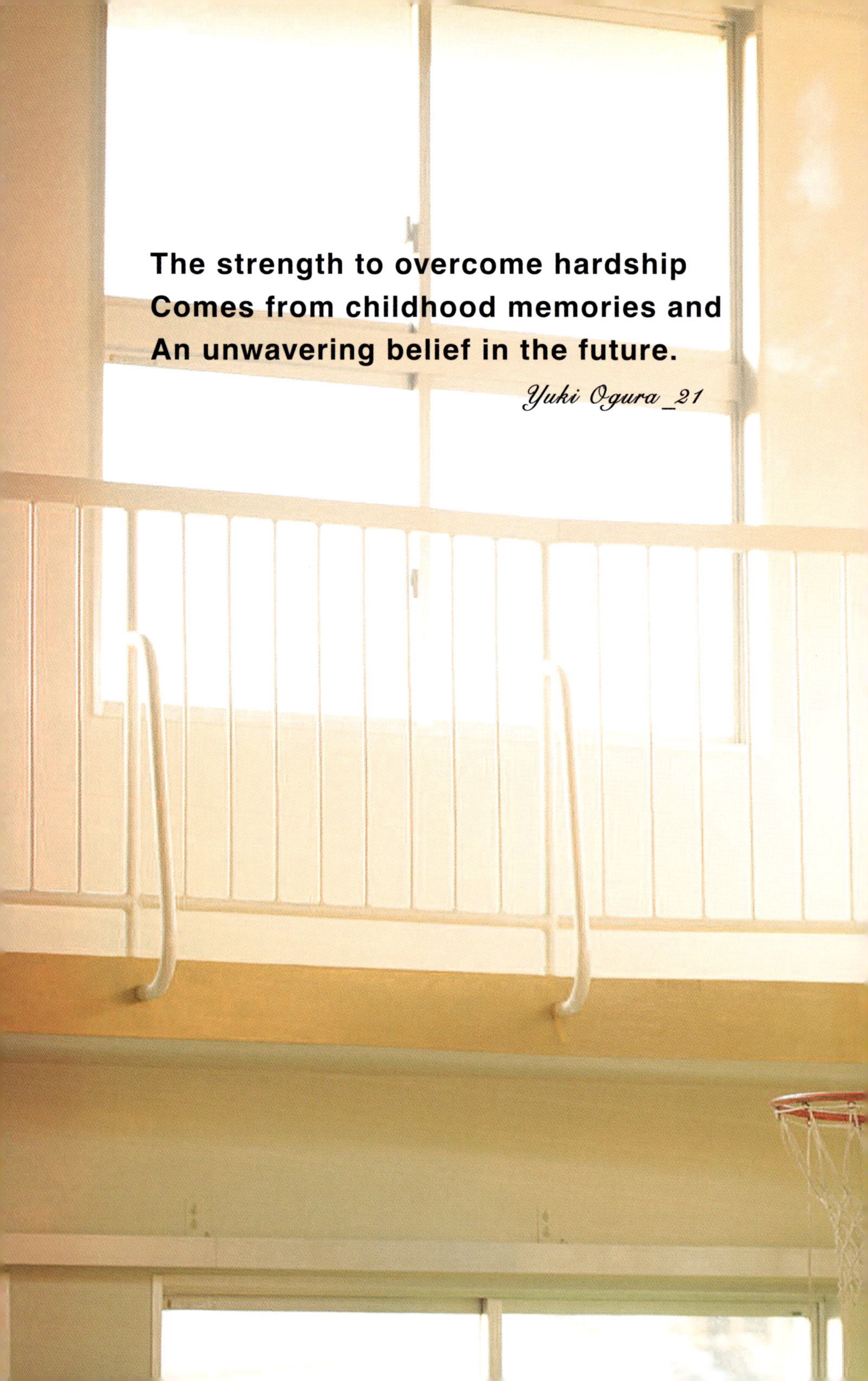
The strength to overcome hardship
Comes from childhood memories and
An unwavering belief in the future.
Yuki Ogura_21

Waka Yuzurihara

Nagasaki

My parents left me With a clear path to follow in life.

I was born the only daughter among three siblings to parents who had married after eloping. My father was the sole heir to a *ryokan* in Hakone. While training at another inn, he met my mother, and despite family opposition, they moved to Nagasaki to start their life together. His work selling seafood and tableware took him all around the country, meaning he wasn't home often. However, whenever he returned, he would bring local gifts, listen attentively to our stories, and shower us with affection. He was truly a wonderful father.

During my middle and high school years, I devoted myself to badminton, competing in prefectural tournaments with considerable dedication. Though I attended an all-girls school, at graduation, I received an outpouring of letters and presents from my female classmates. Looking back, it was probably the day I received the most flowers in my life. I then entered a junior college through a recommendation. I moved into a university dormitory in Kitakyushu. While I certainly applied myself to my studies, the incredible food there was quite distracting. I naturally ended up spending more time at *Izakaya* Japanese pubs, and every night I struggled to make it in before curfew. After graduation, I studied management to help with our family business and worked at various places, including confectionery and select shops. This inability to stay in one place was perhaps my father's blood running through my veins.

Everything changed when my father decided to take over the family business—likely his final gesture of filial piety. He borrowed over one billion yen for reconstruction, while I contributed by doing flower arrangements and using my confectionery skills. However, the timing couldn't have been worse. During the collapse of the bubble economy, we struggled to maintain occupancy. My father's gentle nature made it difficult for him to make the tough decisions required of a business manager. I sometimes expressed my frustrations, but when I did, it created family tensions, and I can still remember the pained expression on my beloved father's face. The situation must have taken a tremendous toll on his mental health.

One day, after what I thought was a casual “Have a good day,” I received word from a hostess that “something terrible has happened to your father.” When I found him, he was already gone. I couldn’t even cry; that’s when I learned that some sorrows run too deep for tears. I was twenty-five years old at the time.

After my father’s passing, our family relationships became strained—disharmony between my paternal grandmother and my mother—as one might expect. Our family relocated to Kyushu, where my mother had become alarmingly thin. However, the return to Kyushu gradually helped her recover her peace of mind. I, on the other hand, moved to Akita and married, though the marriage lasted only two and a half years before I returned. Despite its brevity, it was a valuable experience. I began working in life insurance there and continued after returning to Kyushu. However, I developed skin problems around that time. I became caught in a cycle of steroid dependency—stopping would trigger severe itching. Eventually, I became too self-conscious to meet clients and had to leave the insurance industry.

While working various jobs afterward, a concerned colleague introduced me to INVEL. Though I recognized the products’ quality, I was initially hesitant about making it my career. I attended a seminar, albeit skeptically, thinking it would be pointless. However, during that seminar, I watched a video about eagles and their longevity. At age forty, their first life cycle, they face a trial; only those who overcome it are reborn into a second life. This resonated deeply with me. Here I was in my forties, having lost my father and struggling with health issues, right in the midst of my own trial. I realized it was time to move beyond my first life, where I had been protected by my father. Remembering his words, “Buddha never gives you burdens you can’t bear,” brought me to tears. After nine years of moving between jobs, INVEL became my sole focus.

The beginning wasn't easy. I struggled to effectively communicate with potential business partners. However, I could sense both the quality of Invel products and the genuine integrity of the company and its president. I gradually learned that if I could honestly convey my heartfelt beliefs, that energy would naturally reach others. Indeed, I had felt the products' effectiveness from the start. My initial dedication to INVEL came from wanting my mother to benefit from quality products. She had battled uterine cancer when I was in middle school, followed by colon cancer. She had endured so much while supporting my father. I wanted to show my filial devotion and help maintain her health, which led me to introduce her to Invel products.

Recently, my mother passed away on her eightieth birthday. While she received care in various hospitals and medical facilities, I'm left with some regrets. When I pleaded with the facility where she spent her final days to let her use an Invel mat, they were reluctant to accept it. I desperately tried to convince them, explaining that it was a medically certified product, and eventually managed to at least have them use a blanket. But I can't help thinking that if we had started using it earlier . . . These thoughts continue to haunt me.

That's why I've made a resolution. I want to create a medical facility fully equipped with Invel products. It might seem like an ambitious dream, but I believe this is the path my mother revealed to me throughout her life. As a first step, I'm working with team members to plan a new-style dome salon—a place where people can bring their pets to experience the dome together and enjoy organic vegetable dishes. And after that, I'm determined to pursue my bigger dream. My father provided me with the opportunity for a second life, and my mother showed me the path forward. Together, they left me with clear guidance for my life's journey.

Waka Yuzurihara_22

My parents left me
With a clear path to follow in life.
Waka Yuzurihara_22

Kikumi Oe

Hyogo

When life tests you At your hardest moments, What do you do?

I was born the youngest of four siblings. My father was a cheerful soul who treated everyone equally, without discrimination. My mother was an excellent cook; I can still picture her gentle presence at the kitchen counter. Growing up in this loving family, I was quite pampered. I pursued my passion for oil painting and joined the art department in middle school, with plans to attend art university after high school.

However, fate had other plans. Just before my high school graduation, my father suffered a stroke. He spent the next two years bedridden in the hospital. Our family visited him daily, and my dreams of university faded away. This experience profoundly taught me the value of health—it's actually one of the main reasons I work in healthcare today. My mother ended up caring for my father for twenty-seven years, including providing home care. Since I couldn't solely focus on caregiving, I joined a local company at age twenty, working as an office clerk and learning accounting and insurance. Once I mastered these skills, I felt ready for more customer interaction and transferred to women's clothing sales at a department store. There, I met someone who helped me find my rhythm in life.

My mentor was a striking figure with a sophisticated demeanor and a distinctive black bob cut. They taught a special training program exclusively for top salespeople. Their first lesson stayed with me: "Thoughts become actions, actions become habits, and habits shape character, which ultimately determines your destiny." We underwent intensive training, examining every aspect of our behavior and presence—from having our recorded customer interactions critiqued to receiving feedback on our styling choices. While it was challenging, everything I learned there became invaluable. The results spoke for themselves in our improved sales figures. Determined to succeed, I never missed a weekend shift.

At twenty-six, I married a manufacturer's sales representative. His Kobe posting meant leaving my family in Kyushu, despite my mother's objections. The marriage proved short-lived—I couldn't cope with being a housewife, waiting for a husband who was always traveling nationwide. Looking back, I was probably too young. After divorcing at thirty, I remained in Kobe and found work at a design firm. There, I met my second husband, a highly regarded design department head. We married and soon started our own business.

He had to start finding new customers since he felt it would be stealing to take customers from his previous work. He faced initial struggles but managed to build a successful operation through his combined skills and determination. Then came the inevitable—the Great Hanshin-Awaji Earthquake. While we survived, our business didn't. We accumulated millions of yen in debt, and as a joint guarantor, I continued struggling with monthly repayments even after our eventual divorce.

When the repayments became overwhelming and the divorce happened, I could have chosen bankruptcy. But I believe life's greatest tests reveal our true character in how we respond to them. Instead of running away, I decided to face my challenges head-on. That's when I discovered network marketing.

Though the first few years yielded no results, a breakthrough finally came after about three years of persistence. Even then, I knew success required more than just riding the wave; I needed to grow. During this productive period, I immersed myself in learning, reading over ten books monthly, and attending various self-development seminars. Looking back, I might have gone a bit overboard, but there's no doubt this was a period that built strength in my life.

Through my network of marketing connections, I discovered INVEL, and I still remember my excitement in learning about their Brazilian products coming from across the ocean. Their pitch about the emerging BRIC economies (Brazil, Russia, India, and China) resonated with me, and the product quality spoke for itself. My path became clear. I even traveled to

Brazil for training, where I was captivated by the energy and vitality, especially during Rio's carnival. I could feel my fortunes turning around. I actually attended this training shortly after missing my mother's funeral. When I consulted my brother, he encouraged me: "If this is the path you've chosen, then go for it." So now, I'm determined to succeed, not just for myself, but to become someone who adds value to both the company and its members.

Finally, I've managed to clear all the debt from my joint guarantee, and I've even achieved a top leadership position. From my current perspective, I can see that INVEL is an exceptional organization where even top leaders maintain their drive to grow. Since I dislike my mind and thoughts becoming aged, I'll keep pushing myself forward. However, I believe in doing things my own way. I'm eternally grateful to the members who have believed in me throughout this journey, and I want to show them even more appreciation.

My goal is for us to achieve success together and share the rewards as a team. Moving forward, I want to focus less on monetary gains and more on working for people and creating meaningful memories together. Reflecting on my life, despite the hardships, I'm truly glad I faced every challenge head-on instead of running away. And this is just the beginning. I'm excited to help INVEL grow even bigger with everyone's help.

Kikumi Oe_23

When life tests you
At your hardest moments,
What do you do?
Kikumi Oe_23

Kasumi Nakayama

Hokkaido

The experience of Helping others builds confidence: How your mindset can Transform your life.

My early years in Kitakyushu City weren't particularly happy ones. My parents divorced when I was in first grade, and my mother took my sister and me with her. We lived a nomadic life, changing schools at least seven times—probably more if I counted every move. Though social workers would check on us occasionally, my mother, wary of outside involvement, would simply move us again to avoid government assistance.

She worked nights, leaving me to care for my sister. I struggled to fit in at school or make friends. But amid all this chaos, I found one source of joy: the clarinet, which I picked up in a higher grade. Playing in the band club gave me precious moments of escape, a time when I could forget all my troubles.

In middle school, I threw myself into clarinet practice with my fellow brass band members. Though we narrowly missed gold at competitions, we earned silver medals. Then came another move in my third year, leaving me scrambling to find a new school just before the entrance exams.

My academic strengths got me into a college preparatory high school. I desperately wanted to continue playing clarinet, but the instrument I'd been using had been lent to me by my middle school. High school meant needing my own instrument, and clarinets weren't cheap. I knew I couldn't ask my mother, so I reached out to my father. He turned me down, citing responsibilities to his new family. That rejection sparked a realization in me: I hate being held back by lack of money.

Then came the greatest challenge of my life. My mother was diagnosed with cancer—discovered too late, with doctors giving her just three months to live. This began my journey as her caregiver. I'd go to school during the day, then spend my evenings taking her to hospital appointments and caring for her needs. When the diagnosis came, my sister left home immediately, leaving just my mother and me. Though it was overwhelming, I had no choice; I was all she had. We ended up surpassing the doctor's initial prognosis, and I continued as her caregiver for four years.

While my peers were preparing for university, I had to set aside those dreams. My kind homeroom teacher even offered to help with tuition, saying, "I'll assist with the costs. Please go to university." But with my mother's care and medical expenses to consider, I chose to work instead. I'm eternally grateful to that teacher, who also helped me quickly secure a job.

At twenty, after my mother passed away, I left my job. Around that time, I had an opportunity to connect with an author of a book from which I was highly influenced. My new job was to transcribe lectures into manuscripts for him. Personal computers were just becoming available, so I took classes to learn how to use them. The author would send tapes from Hokkaido to me in Fukuoka, and I'd transcribe and return them. Looking back, it was like an early version of remote work.

At twenty-six, I made a life-changing decision to move to Hokkaido. I'd hoped to work for the author who employed me. Ironically, soon after starting, I conflicted with him. Having spent my childhood constantly moving, I had minimal experience with relationships and struggled with communication. But Hokkaido brought an unexpected blessing—meeting my husband. Something about him made me want to reach out, despite my usual tendency to keep people at arm's length. He proposed shortly after we met, and we quickly married. I had our son when I was thirty, followed by our daughter two years later. My husband's career eventually took us to Tokyo.

At thirty-two, my life took another turn when my husband bought some dietary supplements. When I learned it was network marketing, I was initially skeptical. But the results were remarkable; he lost over ten kilos and even his personality seemed to brighten. Intrigued, I joined him at a presentation where I encountered someone who would change my life—a leader with an infectious smile on stage. They shared how they'd transformed their life from rock bottom to living their dreams, traveling the world freely. Their story made me wonder if I too could change.

At their encouragement, I attended a seminar in Singapore, where I had the privilege of hearing the renowned entrepreneur Jim Rohn speak about how mindset can transform lives. These connections eventually led me to INVEL. After experiencing their products firsthand, I became a true believer. Now I can confidently recommend them to other mothers, and I find many people are eager to learn more.

While the products are remarkable, what truly captivates me is the opportunity to make a difference in people's lives. Being able to help others has become the foundation of my self-confidence. Through INVEL, I've developed a more positive outlook and can now navigate relationships that I once found challenging. I'm deeply grateful for the support of my colleagues and members, and for all the kindness I've received along the way. I'm committed to expanding this wonderful circle of support. My goal is to develop one hundred leaders by the time I'm sixty, and I dream of traveling the world—not just for pleasure, but to spread the message of INVEL globally. To achieve this, I'm determined to maintain my energy and never retire.

When my life comes to an end, I hope to have lived in such a way that I'll be remembered as someone who helped countless people find greater happiness and fulfillment through INVEL.

Kasumi Nakayama_24

The experience of
Helping others builds confidence:
How your mindset can
Transform your life.

Kasumi Nakayama _24

Michie Tsutsumi

Nagasaki

I want to inspire others
By showing them how I live.

I live freely now, but my mother was even more of a free spirit. My earliest memories include a British stepfather. We lived comfortably in Sasebo, Nagasaki, where he worked as a sailor. We had household help, and though my mother would disappear during my father's voyages, my naturally high energy kept me from dwelling on it.

Everything changed in my second year of middle school when my mother moved in with another man and had my half-sister. Rather than join them, I chose to live alone. Despite my young age, I managed a structured life—studying, participating in club activities, playing, handling housework, and even making my own lunches.

This early independence led me to a commercial high school, though I soon transferred to beauty school instead. I'd always enjoyed styling hair, perhaps taking after my mother. But just as I was about to graduate, my mother was diagnosed with atomic-bomb sickness. With a young sister to care for, I helped out at the foreign bar, which was run by my mother's new partner. The pay was good, and I still managed to enjoy my youth, spending time with friends and traveling overseas. A chance street encounter with a high school senior led to a whirlwind marriage at twenty-five. We moved in with my husband's family, who ran a dry-cleaning business, and I opened my own cosmetics shop next door.

With four children, we seemed like the perfect family on the surface. However, tensions with my stepmother never eased, and I struggled to adjust to conventional family life, enduring it all for my children's sake. When I discovered my husband's infidelity at thirty-nine, I knew I'd reached my limit and chose divorce. I restarted my life with my children by purchasing a new house where I could run my own store.

Just a month later, I was diagnosed with cancer. It was already advanced, and with uncertainties about metastasis and future operations, I underwent a nine-hour surgery. Years of stress had taken their toll; I weighed less than 40 kg at the time. My weakened state led to a hospital infection, landing me in intensive care. The following five months of hospitalization were incredibly challenging. I prayed fervently, determined to survive for my children. My older two would cycle to visit me daily, while my mother would bring the younger ones. Their presence gave me the strength to keep fighting.

Perhaps those prayers were heard—even the doctors were amazed by the dramatic drop in my tumor markers—and I was eventually discharged. It showed me the incredible power of determination. However, the journey wasn't over; medication side effects led to depression and panic attacks. Thankfully, friends helped me recover by taking me out to lift my spirits, and I gradually returned to normal life. I was even able to resume working and upgrade my shop from a small apartment room to a location in Sasebo's shopping arcade.

During my recovery, a friend introduced me to network marketing products, suggesting they might help post-illness. Through this connection, I discovered INVEL. I was struggling with my aesthetic services at the time, so I started by introducing their spats. The customer feedback was remarkable; they reported lasting aesthetic effects and reduced waist discomfort. When I tried the spats myself while working, I noticed an improvement in my post-cancer lymphedema. It became clear why these products were used in medical facilities. This led me to recommend them to friends in the same trade and pursue title advancement opportunities. Though I fell slightly short of my target title, this motivated me to attend Tokyo conferences, and gradually, I found my footing.

Realizing my shop management had become inflexible, I decided to focus exclusively on INVEL. Even when faced with the shock of a male partner absconding with funds, I channeled my energy into INVEL. My children were still at an age where they needed educational funds, so I really pushed myself forward. While my children may have felt neglected at times, perhaps witnessing their mother's determination wasn't entirely negative. Now, they're all carving their own impressive paths—some running businesses, others pursuing careers, and one even relocating to New Zealand after studying abroad.

This past May, I spent about six weeks in the hospital. My post-cancer complications—neurogenic bladder and urinary problems—were worsening. While doctors considered it miraculous that I'd managed for twenty years with Invel products' help, learning I'd need self-catheterization felt like my world went dark. But once again, my members lifted me up, reminding me that "every crisis is an opportunity." With their continued support, I've overcome countless obstacles.

Though my body has its limitations now, I'm still moving forward and living a fulfilling life. I believe showing this resilience can inspire others, which gives my journey meaning. I want to spread my wings and soar; that's my dream. To achieve this, I'm dedicated to repaying all the kindness I've received. Currently, I run salons in both Sasebo and Kurume—physical spaces where I can express my gratitude through action. I enjoy daily lunches with members, and here's a fun fact: At night, the salon transforms into "BAR Mitchan," where this mama is always ready to lend an ear to friends in need.

Michie Tsutsumi_25

SIEM COPERNICUS
SIEM COPERNICUS

I want to inspire others
By showing them how I live.

Michie Tsutsumi_25

Kazuko Shirai

Nagasaki

I hope to live to be 100 years old. I'm grateful to INVEL for blessing me With good health and wonderful friends.

I was born in Nishinomiya City, Hyogo, in 1938 and spent my early childhood in Yame City, Fukuoka. I was born before the war. I remember sitting properly in front of the radio during the summer of my first grade when the Emperor's surrender announcement was made. My father, who worked as an engineer at a weapons factory, continued working despite his illness and passed away a year before the war ended. After that, my mother raised me and my two sisters on her own.

As a child, I was a serious student who served as a class representative and did well in my studies. When I helped my friends to complete their homework at their houses, their parents would happily give me vegetables as a token of appreciation. By helping others study, I improved my own academic performance and managed to enter one of the prefecture's prestigious schools. I dreamed of becoming a novelist and wanted to study Japanese literature at university, but when my sister, who wanted to offer financial support, got married, I delisted studying in university from my wish list.

Instead, I enrolled in a tuition-free nursing school in Nagasaki, encouraged by having an uncle there. It was a boarding school. I spent three years studying nursing and living with classmates in the dormitory, but I realized it wasn't quite my calling. Through my public health nursing courses, I discovered my true passion. Becoming a public health nurse required additional schooling and tuition, so I decided to work as a nurse first to save money.

After graduating, I worked at the Osaka Police Hospital. Since I wanted to become a public health nurse specializing in infant care, I requested an assignment to pediatrics. I gained invaluable experience seeing patients in all medical fields, from newborns to elementary school children. During my two years as a nurse, I saved every yen of my salary except for my night shift allowances.

To pursue my public health nursing education, I returned to Nagasaki and lived with my uncle while attending school. Upon graduating, I immediately began working for the Nagasaki City Council. One of my most cherished memories as a public health nurse was being selected as part of the prefectural delegation for a three-week observation tour of America and Canada. This coincided with Japan's preparation to implement its nursing care insurance system, and we went to learn from America's advanced practices. I was one of only two women in the twenty-member delegation, and I was overjoyed when selected. Nagasaki was also the place where I met my husband.

We met at a book club gathering I attended at a friend's invitation. I was twenty-five when we got married. During a trip to the seaside together, my husband suffered a heart attack. I performed a cardiac massage and managed to save his life. I remember thinking that if I had not been with him, he wouldn't have survived. I continued my career after marriage and had three children. My first two were born when I was twenty-five and twenty-seven, and my third, another boy, came after I turned thirty-one. Thanks to a supportive environment, I was able to take maternity leave for each child, and upon returning to work, I balanced childcare and my career with my mother's help. The children were very cooperative too.

As a public health nurse, my primary role was preventive healthcare—keeping healthy people from becoming ill. We developed and implemented various initiatives, including dietary research and educational workshops. I also served as a nursing care insurance certification examiner until my retirement at sixty. Afterward, I continued serving as vice president and standing director of the Japan Nursing Association, remaining actively involved until age seventy, even after retiring from public health nursing.

I was seventy-two, living a peaceful life at the time, when I encountered INVEL. It all started when a friend invited me to hear about something beneficial for my health. At the seminar, they introduced a "futon that provides the same benefits as walking, just by sleeping on it." Finding this remarkable, I first purchased a mat for my husband. He had always had poor health and had to take early retirement from his civil service job at fifty-five due to illness. After he started using INVEL, I noticed him becoming progressively more energetic. *This is truly remarkable*, I thought. When my husband underwent hernia surgery, I tried the mat myself and was amazed by how good it felt. I regretted not getting one for myself sooner and quickly placed another order. Gradually, I started buying them for my children and grandchildren too.

In retrospect, it might have been more economical to buy five at once, but I hadn't studied the business system properly then. When a leader one day suggested I should study it more seriously, I began to understand the structure and found it increasingly interesting. It became almost like a game that I was completely absorbed in. While network marketing doesn't have a great reputation in Japan, I'm so confident in the Invel products that I proudly tell anyone who asks, "I'm involved in network marketing."

The products proved their worth when my husband faced a serious health crisis. What started as a toothache progressed until he couldn't raise his arms. Realizing the severity, we sought emergency care at the duty hospital that Sunday, and after an examination the next day, we were immediately referred to a national hospital. We learned he had developed cerebellar infarction, meningitis, and sepsis from dental bacteria that had spread throughout his body.

The doctor at the hospital told me to prepare myself for the worst-case scenario and asked if I wanted to continue with life-prolonging measures for my husband. I believed in him and brought the Invel mat to his hospital bed. Remarkably, he pulled through the surgery the next day. The doctor was so impressed that he began studying Oriental medicine as a result. Even his prescription approach changed to incorporate Chinese medicine. This experience strengthened my confidence too. It really reinforced my belief in INVEL's effectiveness.

You know, INVEL's philosophy really aligns with public health nursing; it's all about preventing healthy people from becoming ill. During my career as a public health nurse, one of our major challenges was reducing diabetes cases. Once diabetes progresses, patients often require dialysis. I thought, *What if recommending INVEL could help diabetes patients avoid dialysis?* This could help sustain Japan's health insurance system by reducing medical costs. I realized that through INVEL, even in retirement, I could continue contributing to society.

INVEL has truly blessed me in many ways. While there are certainly health and financial benefits, friendships are what I value most. Even people I've just met feel like longtime friends. These relationships are truly precious. I want to continue with INVEL until I am one hundred. The fact that we seniors can maintain our health and vitality is itself a contribution to society. I'm eighty-five now, so please come back and interview me again in fifteen years when I'm one hundred.

Kazuko Shirai_26

I hope to live to be 100 years old.
I'm grateful to INVEL for blessing me
With good health and wonderful friends.

Mieko Tomiyasu

Fukuoka

I was once unable to Study or exercise, My body was weak, And my spirit was defeated.

My personality as a child was completely different from who I am today. I was painfully shy, always hiding behind my mother. My father was an alcoholic who spent nearly his entire salary on drinking, while my mother worked late into the night to support us. We were poor, as you might expect. Even with the lights on, our rooms seemed perpetually dark. I would sit in that darkness each night, silently waiting for my mother to return.

At school, I was practically invisible. I couldn't keep up with my studies or sports, and I constantly tried to avoid swimming classes. Though I had a stubborn streak, my physical weakness was overwhelming. I couldn't even sit at a desk for extended periods. When people ask me about happy memories from my school days, I draw a complete blank.

My first job after high school was at a local bank in Fukuoka. Though it was an office position, even sitting in a chair was a struggle. My mother sternly told me, "Just stick it out for three years! A rolling stone gathers no moss." I managed to endure exactly that long before resigning. I then moved to a door-to-door cosmetics sales company, starting again in an office role. Watching the saleswomen return to the office excitedly saying things like, "I made 100,000 yen in sales today!" made me think, *Perhaps I could do that too.* While talking to strangers was initially daunting, once I framed it as "just work," I surprisingly found my voice. However, the job came to an abrupt end when a customer had a seizure and lost consciousness during one of my cosmetics demonstrations. The incident left me traumatized, and I couldn't continue in cosmetics sales. I then spent many years working at an apparel shop in a local department store, but during those two decades, I would face my greatest challenge yet.

At age thirty-nine, I was diagnosed with rheumatoid arthritis. It started with one knee swelling to triple its normal size, then spread to my wrists. When blood tests confirmed it was rheumatoid arthritis, I was absolutely devastated. Seeing the patients with advanced rheumatoid arthritis in the waiting room, my world went dark as I realized, "This is my future. I'll be confined to a wheelchair."

The first half of my forties became a blur of painkillers and deteriorating health. The intervals between pain episodes grew shorter and shorter until eventually even the simple act of walking became agonizing. I tried everything imaginable—Chinese tea, health supplements, any potential remedy—but nothing made a real difference. I spent most of my days off simply lying in bed. Even though I found emotional support after meeting my current husband at age forty-nine, there was no relief from the relentless rheumatoid pain. The condition wasn't just destroying my body anymore; it was beginning to break my spirit as well. That's the desperate situation I found myself in.

Then, at age fifty-six, a ray of hope pierced through the dark clouds of my despair. My encounter with Invel products marked the beginning of my pain's disappearance. A colleague introduced me to them, and after hearing the explanation, I immediately believed in their potential. I purchased both sleepwear and daywear items and surrounded myself with Invel products. While there was no change for the first twenty days or so, after about a month, the pain suddenly vanished. It was both astonishing and liberating. Living without pain—something I hadn't experienced in over a decade—made everything seem brighter, both literally and figuratively.

The network business aspect, which I initially thought would be beyond my capabilities, gave me something I'd lost long ago: the ability to dream of goals like "achieving success" or "visiting Hawaii." I had resigned myself to spending my life in a dark room, just enduring pain, believing I would never have dreams or goals again. Yet once I became involved with Invel's activities, I—someone who could never study or exercise—found myself achieving goals one after another. Though I once thought nearby hot

springs would be the extent of my travel, I've now been to Hawaii six times! What struck me most about joining INVEL was finding like-minded, motivated friends. While I'd had work colleagues before, they would often gather just to complain about the company or gossip about others. I had accepted this negativity as normal. But INVEL is different; it's full of positive people who enjoy life and share ambitious dreams, such as "becoming number one in Japan." I never imagined I could make such new friendships at this stage of my life, and for this too, I'm grateful to INVEL.

Looking back, Invel products are truly products of light. They bring happiness to those who use them and inspire dreams. While hospitals can provide medicine for physical ailments, they can't offer the kind of life guidance that teaches you how to live with a positive mindset. In my case, encountering INVEL hasn't just changed my life—it has transformed my entire personality. While I used to prefer traveling alone in the past, now I suddenly find myself enjoying traveling with Invel friends.

I'm genuinely excited to see how both INVEL and I will continue to grow. While I'm working toward achieving the highest title, I have even bigger dreams beyond that. I want to help drill one hundred wells in Africa and other developing regions! I've learned it costs 300,000 yen to drill one well, so I'm working to earn enough to donate 30 million yen. When I heard that there are children in Africa whose dream is to grow to become an adult, it really struck a chord with me. Having spent so many years without dreams or goals myself, I feel compelled to do something for these children. The fact that I can now dream of making such social contributions is all thanks to INVEL. It's amazing to think that I—someone who couldn't study or exercise, who was weak and suffering from rheumatoid arthritis, who had given up on everything—could experience such a complete transformation in life!

Mieko Tomiyasu_27

I was once unable to
Study or exercise,
My body was weak,
And my spirit was defeated.

Mieko Tomiyasu _27

Takako Nozoe

Oita

Even when poor,
Even when suffering,
I never gave up.

I was born in Miyazaki City, Miyazaki. My father worked for the prefectural government, and my mother was a gentle soul—like a goddess with her ever-present smile. We were a family of six, including my siblings and me, and until financial worries set in, we lived comfortably without any real concerns.

Everything changed when I was in first grade. My father suffered a stroke that left him hemiplegic, and our lives were transformed overnight. My childhood memories are steeped in poverty. We wore hand-me-downs and ill-fitting discount shoes. We used our school supplies—notebooks and pencils—with utmost care, making them last as long as possible. Despite these circumstances, I excelled academically. Though my father could no longer work after his stroke, his passion for education never wavered, and he continued to teach me.

Driven by an especially strong determination not to be defeated by our circumstances, I maintained my academic efforts through middle and high school while helping care for my father. Yet reality can be cruel. Even with top grades, society and employers tend to favor those from stable home environments. I faced many moments of bitter disappointment. Nevertheless, refusing to give up, I persevered, and after high school graduation, I secured a position at Nippon Telegraph and Telephone Public Corporation (now NTT).

At age twenty-two, while working at NTT, I met the man who would become my husband. He came from a respected family in Bungotakada City, Oita. He seemed almost too good to be true for someone like me. Yet once again, family circumstances would put us to the test. His grandmother strongly opposed our marriage, declaring, "We cannot accept someone from such a family as a spouse for our grandchild." Those words brought back that familiar sting of discrimination. But this time was different; I didn't have to face it alone. My future husband stood up to his grandmother, telling her through tears, "I've been blessed with a comfortable upbringing. That's exactly why I need someone like Takako, who understands life's hardships." Watching him defend our love so earnestly, I thought to myself, *At last, my champion has arrived*, and felt truly blessed. We married when I was twenty-four.

Just when happiness seemed complete, another challenge emerged. At age twenty-six, I contracted Hepatitis C from a blood transfusion during the birth of my first child. From then on, my body was constantly fatigued. However, determined not to return to the poverty of my youth, I continued working at NTT while raising my children. Balancing housework with raising three children was incredibly demanding, but with my husband's help, we managed to get through each day.

At thirty-four, I resigned from NTT to move to Oita, where my husband was transferred to. At thirty-six, I began working in door-to-door cosmetics sales. While my husband maintained steady employment, my personal experience with illness made me anxious about not working. I started this new career at the suggestion of a neighbor from our company housing complex. I ended up staying in cosmetics sales for fifteen years and found I had a genuine aptitude for it. Despite occasionally feeling drained by the interpersonal dynamics of an all-female workplace, I consistently maintained top-level sales performance, even achieving national first-place rankings several times.

However, age and illness began taking their toll. Living with Hepatitis C, my health deteriorated, and door-to-door sales became increasingly challenging. At fifty-one, I transitioned to network business. Unlike door-to-door sales, which is essentially like running a one-person shop, network businesses offer companionship. Having colleagues made a remarkable difference, even in studying product information—the motivation was completely different than working alone. I continued this for about five years. This period coincided with our three children attending university and graduate school. Even our combined incomes weren't sufficient to cover the expenses. We managed day by day, borrowing from various sources to make ends meet.

I discovered INVEL during this period. When someone from my network business sideline invited me to a seminar, I decided to give it a try. The seminar was remarkably plain; even the presentation style was rather basic. But that turned out to be a blessing. The products had an inherent appeal, and unlike my previous network business in cosmetics, where I had to maintain a polished appearance with makeup, INVEL didn't require such a superficial presentation. I instinctively felt that this was something sustainable. While financial motivation initially drew me in, the first changes I noticed were physical.

Within about three months of using the products, I began experiencing benefits. My circulation improved noticeably, and my issues with constipation and cold sensitivity disappeared. After six months, my body had transformed so dramatically that it made me question the effectiveness of all my previous treatments and health supplements. Even my chronic fatigue had vanished. When I introduced it to my family, they became enthusiastic supporters. Even my children, who had opposed my previous network business ventures, became encouraging. Gradually, our financial situation also improved.

Meeting this company was truly a divine gift. Now at seventy-one, I'm still setting higher goals while steadily saving for family trips to Hawaii and retirement. Reflecting on my journey, I want to share with everyone that despite periods of poverty and hardship, perseverance opens doors to the future. Today, I'm experiencing joy in life like never before.

Takako Nozoe_28

Even when poor,
Even when suffering,
I never gave up.
Takako Nozoe_28

Shinako Suzuki

Okinawa

Looking back, I realized I was always surrounded By smiling faces.

I grew up on Minami Daito Island, about four hundred kilometers from Okinawa's main island, in a family that farmed sugarcane. As one of six siblings—with two older sisters, two younger brothers, and a younger sister—I spent my days helping with the younger ones and tending to our livestock when at home. While my father was quite strict, my mother was incredibly gentle.

At fifteen, following in my older sisters' footsteps, I moved to the main island of Okinawa to attend high school. It was my first experience living alone. Life in Naha offered a welcome reprieve from my father's strict oversight, though homesickness still crept in. In those days before mobile phones, I would often find myself at public phone booths, clutching 10-yen coins and calling home just to hear my mother's voice. When others would line up behind me, I'd hang up only to rejoin the queue. Despite desperately wanting to return home, I never voiced this desire, especially when my mother would encourage me, saying, "Shinako, you're doing so well."

After graduating high school and starting work in Naha, my brother, three years younger than me, came over from Minami Daito Island. Though I had sisters and relatives on the main island, I volunteered to look after him. Perhaps it was because I didn't want him to experience the loneliness I had felt, or maybe I wanted to get praised by my parents. Instead of going out after work, I would head straight home to our apartment, cook dinner for him, and share stories about our day.

I was twenty when I first got married. My husband, a cook at the same workplace where I worked, and I had a child together. While he was a good person at heart, we had my brother living with us at the time, and I believe my husband was harboring various frustrations. Being young myself, I struggled to handle the emotional complexity of the situation, and gradually, our relationship began to deteriorate. The stress of our situation took its toll on our five-year-old child, who developed alopecia areata.

Despite this, I couldn't bring myself to tell the truth to anyone—not the doctors, not the people around me. When asked if our family was happy, I would simply respond, "Yes, we're happy." I maintained this facade, though it was perhaps the most challenging period of my life. While I was crying inside, I kept a smile on my face and pretended everything was fine. Eventually, I confided in my sister and asked if we could live with her temporarily. This change proved beneficial: My child's condition improved, and when my brother graduated from high school, I took the opportunity to discuss divorce with my husband. In the end, I chose to build a new life with just my child and me.

Later, around the time my child entered middle school, I met Suzuki, who would become my current partner. I had convinced myself I would never marry again, yet before I knew it, the three of us were living together as a family. When it came time to help look after my sister's children at our house, Suzuki stepped forward during my moments of struggle, saying, "Let's take care of them together at our home." Though I felt apologetic about the situation, I was incredibly touched.

I look back now with love—whether it was the three of us who left my family home, my eldest son from my previous marriage, my eldest daughter with Suzuki, or my sister's children. While it might sound odd coming from me, I believe I've really done my part in caring for others. Ever since I made my decision to discover my honest views and drop my public facade when my eldest son was five, we've managed to get through every difficulty without bottling things up, even though life has certainly had its challenges.

I was introduced to INVEL when my husband, Suzuki, developed an interest in their products. Initially, I was skeptical about network marketing businesses and doubted their effectiveness. But I couldn't deny the results: The gloves made my hands beautiful, the spats reduced cellulite, and the belt created noticeable changes around my waist. "What! This is a lie!"

I was so amazed that I actually took my first-ever unauthorized day off from my part-time job and soon found myself enthusiastically introducing the products to my friends. However, we faced unique challenges with the Suzuki surname. In Okinawa, having a typical mainland Japanese surname like Suzuki often raised suspicions. To demonstrate our commitment to the community, we built a house here, I became actively involved in our daughter's school PTA, and I participated extensively in local volunteer work.

Now, thirteen years after joining INVEL, we've established a dome salon just a few seconds' drive from our home. Both my children have grown into remarkable adults. I believe nothing makes children happier than seeing their parents full of vitality. While we've certainly faced our share of hardships, I'm blessed with family and relatives who keep my spirits high, along with Invel members who have become like a second family.

These days, my nephews and nieces visit and playfully call me "Shinā" (my nickname), and my brothers who returned to Minami Daito Island send us local specialties. And, of course, there's my husband. With all this support, I feel I can face any challenge that comes my way.

As for my future dreams, I hope to wear Invel brand clothing and walk down a fashion show runway. I envision seeing INVEL's magnificent designs become a major trend, with people throughout the streets wearing the same brand. When I think back to when I was fifteen, just having left Minami Daito Island, I was completely alone, filled with anxiety and loneliness. Now, I find myself surrounded by the smiling faces of so many wonderful people.

Life, I've learned, is about this beautiful reciprocity—when you look after others and support them, you end up being cared for and supported in return. It's a continuous cycle of giving and receiving energy. This is something I've come to believe in deeply.

Looking back,
I realized I was always surrounded
By smiling faces.
Shinako Suzuki_29

Acknowledgments

To my Mama, Satiko Taba, a Brazilian Japanese woman,
the eldest daughter of immigrants,
now ninety-one years old and living in Japan. Her wisdom, faith,
and indomitable spirit flow through our family like
an invisible thread, sustaining our work, business ventures,
and social contributions. She built the foundation
with quiet strength and unwavering determination.

About the Author

Carla Taba is a third-generation Japanese–Brazilian entrepreneur and cultural bridge-builder who has dedicated her career to fostering connections between Brazil and Japan through business and community engagement. As CEO of INVEL, she has spent over two decades building relationships between the two countries while championing the wisdom and strength of Japanese women. Born and raised in Brazil with deep Japanese roots, Taba brings a unique perspective to understanding the experiences of Japanese women navigating tradition and modernity. She is a mother of four, an attorney, and a businesswoman who draws inspiration from her Japanese–Brazilian mother's remarkable journey as an educator and entrepreneur.